Claude Cahun

Introduction by François Leperlier

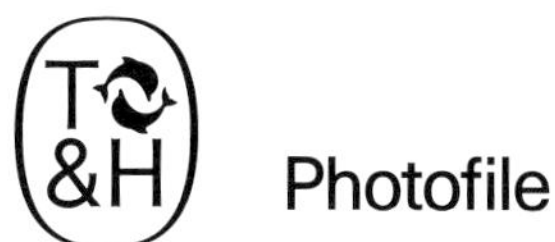

Photofile

Note

This book refers to Claude Cahun with the she/her
pronouns that she used during her own lifetime.

The Staged Eye

Unrecognized for many years, the photographic work of Claude Cahun has become the object of striking, even extraordinary attention since the 1990s. This has included retrospectives at the Institute of Contemporary Arts in London (1994), the Musée d'Art Moderne de la Ville de Paris (1995), Ginza Artspace in Tokyo (1997), the Pinakothek in Munich (1997), the Jeu de Paume in Paris (2011) and the Kunsthal in Rotterdam (2022). It should be remembered that the monograph that made this artist widely known was published in 1992. I was able to make an inventory of Claude Cahun's archives, which were acquired at a public sale in Jersey, shortly after the death of her partner Suzanne Malherbe (Marcel Moore) in February 1972. The sort of rapture with which she was greeted by young critics and tastemakers (most notably, several designers claimed that her work had inspired their collections) confirms the attraction that she still exerts today on the world of shifting ideas and morality.

What would have constituted a disadvantage during Claude Cahun's lifetime seemed to be a boon in this new context: here was a woman who never stopped questioning her identity and experimenting with self-representation, who displayed huge freedom in her political, intellectual and sexual choices, who asserted her 'eclecticism' and crossed boundaries of gender and genre to build a body of work that was literary, theatrical, sculptural and photographic. Before leaving Paris in 1937, she had held small exhibitions, dinners and get-togethers at her studio that were attended by some of the leading figures of intellectual life, including Henri Michaux, Robert Desnos, André Breton, Tristan Tzara, Georges Bataille, Man Ray and René Crevel. She also played an active but deliberately discreet part in the great causes of her time, especially those that involved moral emancipation, social revolution, poetic subversion and the fight against Nazism.

The impact of this rediscovery seemed as sizeable as the neglect that had previously been bestowed upon her work. Admittedly, she did nothing to bring it to public attention – she called it her 'invisible adventure' – but we must also keep in mind the loss of a large portion of her archives and photographic works in the wake of her arrest by the German police in Jersey in 1944, and the raiding of her home.

Its thematic originality and its wealth of formal innovations make Claude Cahun's body of work a key moment in the aesthetics of modernity. It is a milestone in both the Surrealist conquest of the photographic image and the history of Surrealism itself (to which Claude Cahun was closely linked), while also broadly anticipating contemporary experiments in the genre (from Cindy Sherman to Alain Fleischer).

Claude Cahun said very little about the activity that started early (in around 1912) and lasted, with periods of great intensity, for her entire life. In her letters, she made reference to irreparable losses, to the destruction of her 'best shots' during the war. It is known that she gave prints to a few friends, and presented some to bookshops (including those owned by Adrienne Monnier, Sylvia Beach and José Corti), but it was not until 1937, with the twenty-two tableaux for *Le Coeur de Pic*,[1] that her photographic work truly took on a public dimension. The self-portrait published in *Bifur* (no. 5, April 1930) had remained a one-off and the photomontages created for her autobiographical essay, *Aveux non avenus*, were still virtually unseen. In 1952, she considered, without much conviction, getting some images included in works published by the Guilde du Livre, in Switzerland. Once again, as previously, she rejected any kind of specialization and the very idea of a career. Nonetheless, despite the great modesty she displayed, she was able to find genuine compensations. She wrote in 1951: 'From the pre-war period (Paris and Jersey), we still have some rather fine photographs. Fine? If I can judge by the diverse range of people who have admired them...

strangers when they were exhibited in bookshops… and by the
admiration of some of those who saw them in our home. They ranged
from the least aesthetic of people to professionals such as Man Ray.
What's more, recently, a young Englishman, another professional […],
asked us questions about "innovation" (!) and techniques (!)…
regarding our amateur attempts dating from more than a quarter
of a century ago.'[2]

Clues to the contemporary reception of Claude Cahun's works
are fairly rare. A letter from Paul Éluard, about the images for *Le Coeur
de Pic*: 'Your photographs are ideal for the poems of *L'Heure des fleurs*,[3]
pure wonders that appeal to what still remains childlike within
us […]. I believe that the book will be ready on time […] and that it
will be *the finest book of the year*.' There is also a brief note from Gaston
Ferdière: 'Claude Cahun created a worthy setting for these pieces,
in the form of a splendid series of photomontages….'[4]

The technical demands of her work were so closely entwined
with her poetic approach that she never drew attention to them, but
the ingenuity and sophistication of some of the images nevertheless
display a great understanding of the medium. As much as she loathed
the process when exploited for its own sake, she also loved to explore
the potential of photographic expression, both in terms of genres
(self-portrait, staged objects, snapshot, photomontage, *tableaux vivants*)
and processes (symmetry, mirrors, distortion, insertion, overlaying,
retouching). From a letter from Youki Desnos, it is known that
she had a small darkroom on the rue Notre-Dame-des-Champs –
and probably had access to another in Nantes – where, with the
collaboration of her partner, Suzanne Malherbe, prints were made
that required skilful manipulation. But she also used professional
developing labs, including Pearl, on the rue Bréa.

Free from any commercial or professional considerations,
the photographic work of Claude Cahun, in its very diversity,
is the product of a meticulously considered poetics that follows
its own rules and is striking for its extraordinary originality.
By favouring staged images – whether of herself (self-portraits),
other people (portraits), objects (photographic tableaux) or
symbols (photomontages) – she uses photography as part of

an intimate, existential and poetic experiment, whose motifs are explained at length in her literary work, and which had the goal of destabilizing the perception of reality and emphasizing the power of the imagination. She must have been aware of the work of her contemporaries, such as Man Ray, Jacques-André Boiffard, Brassaï, and those who collaborated with *Bifur* (André Kertész, Germaine Krull, Eli Lotar, Maurice Tabard), but any search for direct influences or borrowings would be fruitless. Among the Surrealists, Claude Cahun was closest to Man Ray. The dedication she wrote to him on her pamphlet *Les paris sont ouverts* ('to Man Ray, with my very great sympathy') tells us virtually nothing about their relationship. Nonetheless, it is apparent that he admired her experiments. While their approaches were very distinct, one cannot help but observe certain formal similarities that seem to indicate that special attention has been paid to the work of Claude Cahun – although the dates may not always be convincing. These include the regular use of glass bell jars as methods of 'enclosure', small wooden mannequins, and certain parallels in the way objects are arranged.

For almost forty years, Claude Cahun created self-portraits. This is the genre she explored most widely, the one that engaged with the most powerful issues and that still exerts an incomparable fascination. Never before in the history of photography had the questioning of identity, the answer to 'who am I?', been pursued so extensively and with such intensity. There is nothing anecdotal here; the staging is reduced to a minimum: a section of wall, a piece of rock, a stretched piece of cloth or a dense mass of flowers to close off the space and centre the body or the face. Only a reflecting surface will replace the background, enabling an endlessly repeating dialogue:

    '*Between my mirror and my body, shorten the leash.*

    And now onto we two.'[5]

Whether dressing up, playing with masks or stripping bare, Claude Cahun never stopped casting herself in roles, creating more and more images of herself until she reached the boundaries of that 'indefinite' sexuality that she dreamed of turning into a third gender. In fact, she aspired towards a transformation, a transfiguration of all genders and

genres – homosexuality, bisexuality, androgyny – in order to assert
her own, which could not be reduced to any other. 'Individualism?
Narcissism? Of course. That's my best feature.' This radical atypicality
placed her beyond the reach of ideologically charged reclamation
of any kind, including feminist. She would never be anywhere other
than on 'her own side', which always meant 'the other side', where
she was not expected but where she could find herself even through
self-inflicted violence. She was her own executioner and her own
demiurge. A doll, a model young lady, a tomboy, a demon, a virgin,
a martyr, an angel, a monster, a priestess, a fairy… 'The happiest
moments of my life? Dreams. Imagining that I'm somebody else.
Acting out my favourite role.' Her baroque exhibitionism, love of
makeup, elevation of the obscene, theatrical cruelty, exaggerated
dandyism – they were all indictments of nature itself. She had to tear
herself away from immediacy and necessity, and ultimately remake
a body for herself, an imaginary body – whether by subtraction
('There is too much of everything […]. I shall shave off my hair, tear
out my teeth, my breasts – everything that annoys or tires my gaze –
the stomach, the ovaries, the conscious and cyst-filled brain') or by
accumulation ('Lauding the imagination of the costume designer').
Poetry and art had never pushed so hard against nature. 'Nothing but
artifice in me, so little that's primal.' Nature, like the human body
itself, is only precious for its flaws, its differences, its vagaries, for the
space it allows for metaphorical reworking and metamorphosis. We
might see this as a truly Baudelairean idea (only Claude Cahun could
have reconciled Baudelaire with photography!). From here springs
the provocation that she does not deliberately seek but which she
wields like an artform, as if in a dream… There is a 'spectacular' form
of evasiveness that is both withdrawal and challenge, concealment
and power. At the root of this interplay of masculine and feminine
imagery, otherness and androgyny, monstrous beauty and sublime
ugliness, at the heart of this tension lies the conquest of the self
through what is greater and stronger than the self, the frantic quest
for a personal myth in which the subject becomes its own source
of imagination, its own poetic object. 'Myself alone, at last. Naked
haste…' The risk of forced comparisons must nonetheless be avoided.

Of course, it's impossible not to be reminded of the photographic work of Pierre Molinier, Gina Pane, Francesca Woodman, Urs Lüthi, or indeed Cindy Sherman. But any connections that can be observed in terms of formal expression or narcissistic affirmation should not be allowed to overshadow the differences in aesthetic approaches. For example, the sociological concept of 'switching roles', in order to portray a range of stereotypes, which takes on a systematic quality in the work of Cindy Sherman, is utterly foreign to the poetic metamorphosis of the self in the work of Claude Cahun, in which the varying forms of otherness all spring from an exoticism that is entirely interior.

Most of the elements from which the photomontages are made come from the self-portraits. Claude Cahun drew from this source as if it were a 'monstrous dictionary of analogies/antagonisms', in the words of Hans Bellmer. Each image, with its icon-like composition, is a visual metaphor in which the rituals of the inner quest are made and unmade, ranging from family sagas to dreams of another life. These are stark affirmations of the extreme recentring of the will, creating mutated versions of her self-portraits until she becomes her own object of worship and repulsion. The ambivalence of the idol.

The earliest photomontages seem to date from around 1926, six years before Claude Cahun became acquainted with the Surrealists. With the skilful and inspired collaboration of her partner, Suzanne Malherbe, who is probably responsible for their striking three-dimensional quality, she went on to create some of the most unusual and striking compositions of this 'golden age' of collage. If we precede with caution, it could be useful to compare the pieces that illustrate *Aveux non avenus* with works by Hannah Höch or Raoul Hausmann (the inclusion of self-portraits) or, better still, with a particular tone found in Giorgio de Chirico or Max Ernst. During the war, Claude Cahun may well have recalled the works of John Heartfield, which she had the opportunity to see in Paris in 1935. She created many photomontages, this time political in intent, focusing on indirect action and aiming to spoof the German illustrated press in an ironic, defeatist and anti-militaristic way.

Most of the portraits taken by Claude Cahun are evidence of close relationships: Suzanne Malherbe, Sylvia Beach, Henri Michaux, Robert Desnos, André and Jacqueline Breton. Here once again, she favoured 'mirror' compositions that required 'skilful handiwork' – repurposed images, double exposures, overprinted negatives – and marked a dual desire: to depict the inner duality of the subject ('homo duplex', in the words of Baudelaire), and to use her model as a willing medium for projection or appropriation. To paraphrase Claude Cahun, it could be argued that the leash between the photographer and the model must always be shortened!

We have grouped together all assemblages of objects under the heading 'photographic tableaux', playing on the double meaning of the word 'tableau': theatrical (staged scenes) and pictorial (three-dimensional compositions). Beginning in the mid-1920s, this experimentation culminated in twenty-two plates to illustrate the poetry book *Le Coeur de Pic*. Its publication occurred soon after the exhibition at the Charles Ratton gallery, for which Claude Cahun had made and photographed several objects with what Surrealism would term 'symbolic functions'. These 'tableaux' are based on ephemeral arrangements of found or specially produced objects, often in a natural setting (a garden, a beach). True visual poems, they are an invitation both to interpret and to dream. This 'photographic concept', once so little used that we might conclude that Claude Cahun invented it, could be found only rarely at the time in the work of Man Ray. It came to its fullest expression in the work of Hans Bellmer, whose *Les Jeux de la Poupée* (1934–1939) used allegory to perform a kind of ritual of possession.

Despite the disparity in their temperaments, Claude Cahun and Bellmer shared some deep poetic affinities. From later years, we might discern similarities with the images created by Jindřich Štyrský (most notably *On the Needles of These Days*, 1941), or with some of the output of animated filmmakers (Jan Lenica, Ladislas Starevich), though without any evidence of direct influence.

The boom in staged photography in recent years seems to have broadly confirmed Claude Cahun's intuition. Think, for example, of the 'installations' of Bernard Faucon, Annette Messager, Christian Boltanski or Alain Fleischer. In the photographic tableaux, as in the portraits and self-portraits, Claude Cahun wanted to associate photography with the staging of appearances, as if that was where its essence lay. Breaking away from the art of representation, or illusion, Claude Cahun boldly incorporated the photographic act into a kind of transfiguration of sensory experience, a poetics of metamorphosis – 'The impossible made real through a magic mirror.'

François Leperlier

Notes

1   Lise Deharme, *Le Coeur de Pic*, 20 photographs by Claude Cahun, foreword by Paul Éluard, Paris: José Corti, 1937.
2   Claude Cahun, letter to Charles-Henri Barbier, 6–21 September 1952.
3   This was the original title that was changed to *Le Coeur de Pic*.
4   Gaston Ferdière, 'Le Coeur de Pic', *L'École émancipée*, no. 29, 18 April 1937.
5   Claude Cahun, *Aveux non avenus*, Paris: Éditions du Carrefour, 1930. All subsequent quotes are taken from this edition.

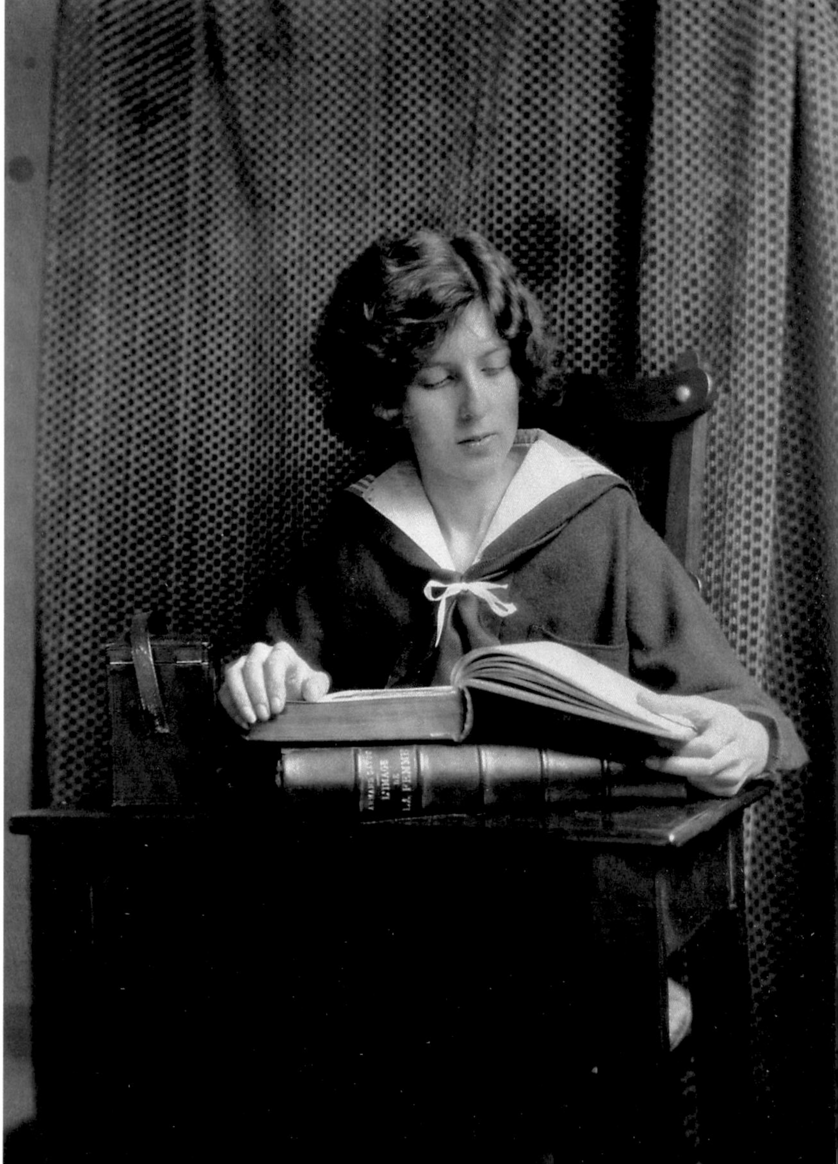

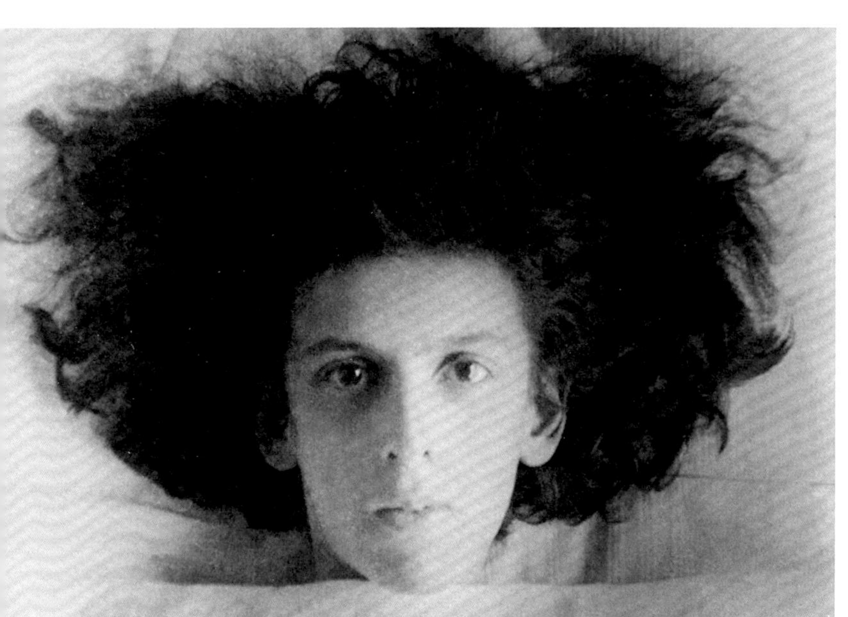

1. 1915.

2. c. 1914.

3. c. 1917.

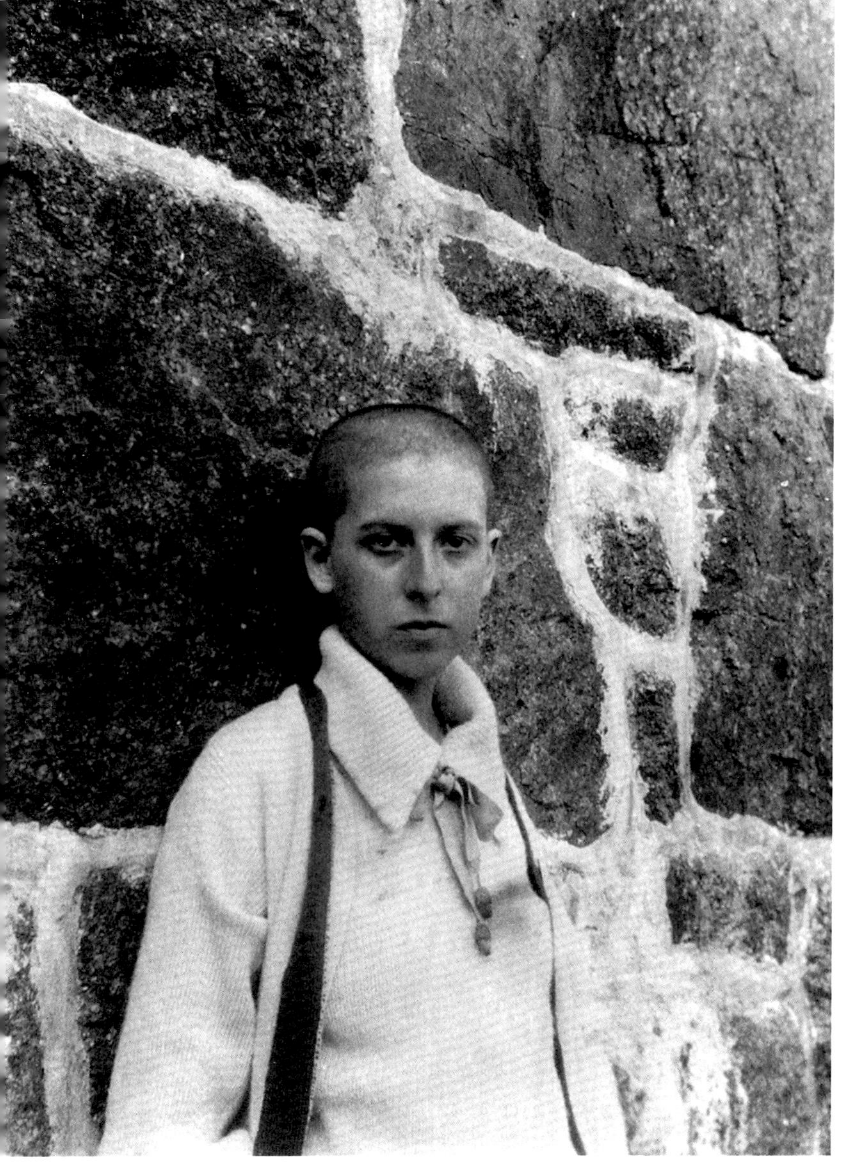

4.1928.

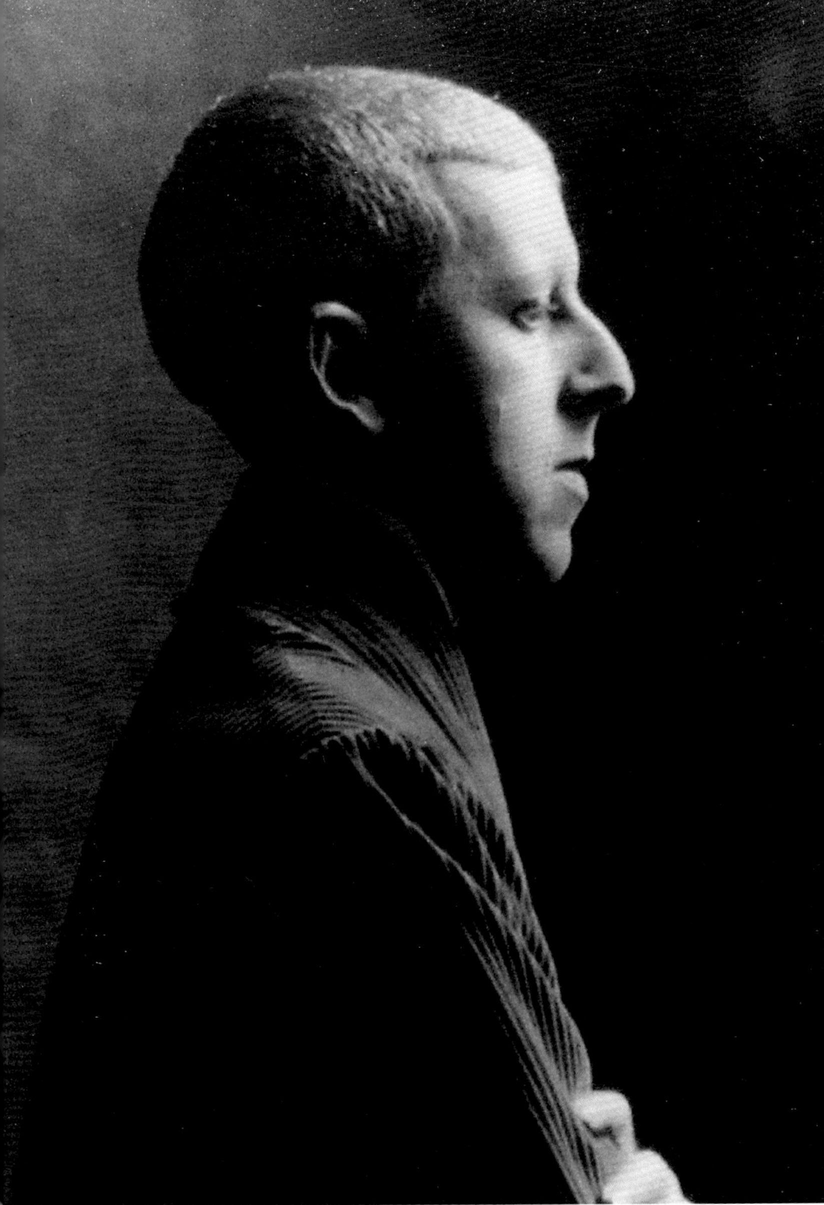

5. c. 1920.

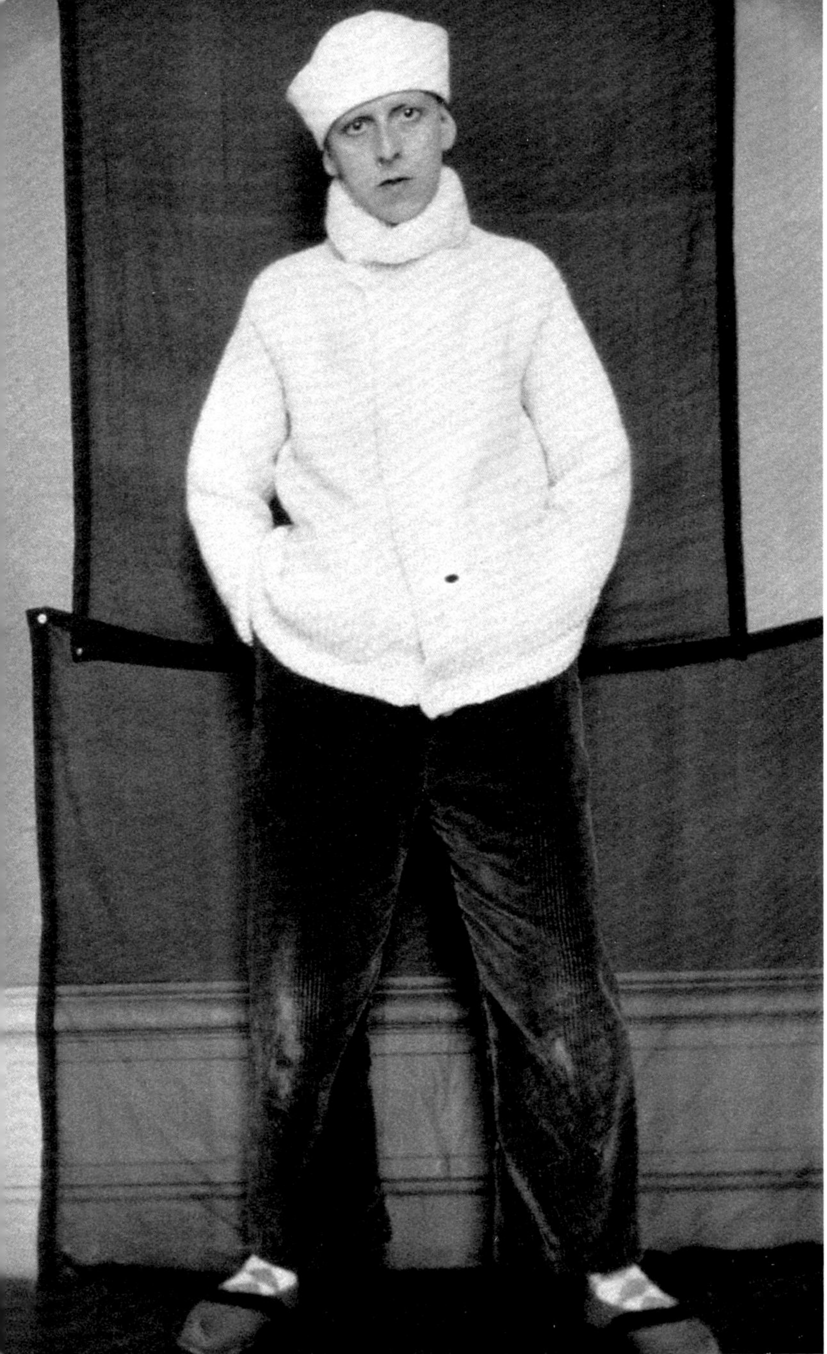

6. c. 1920.

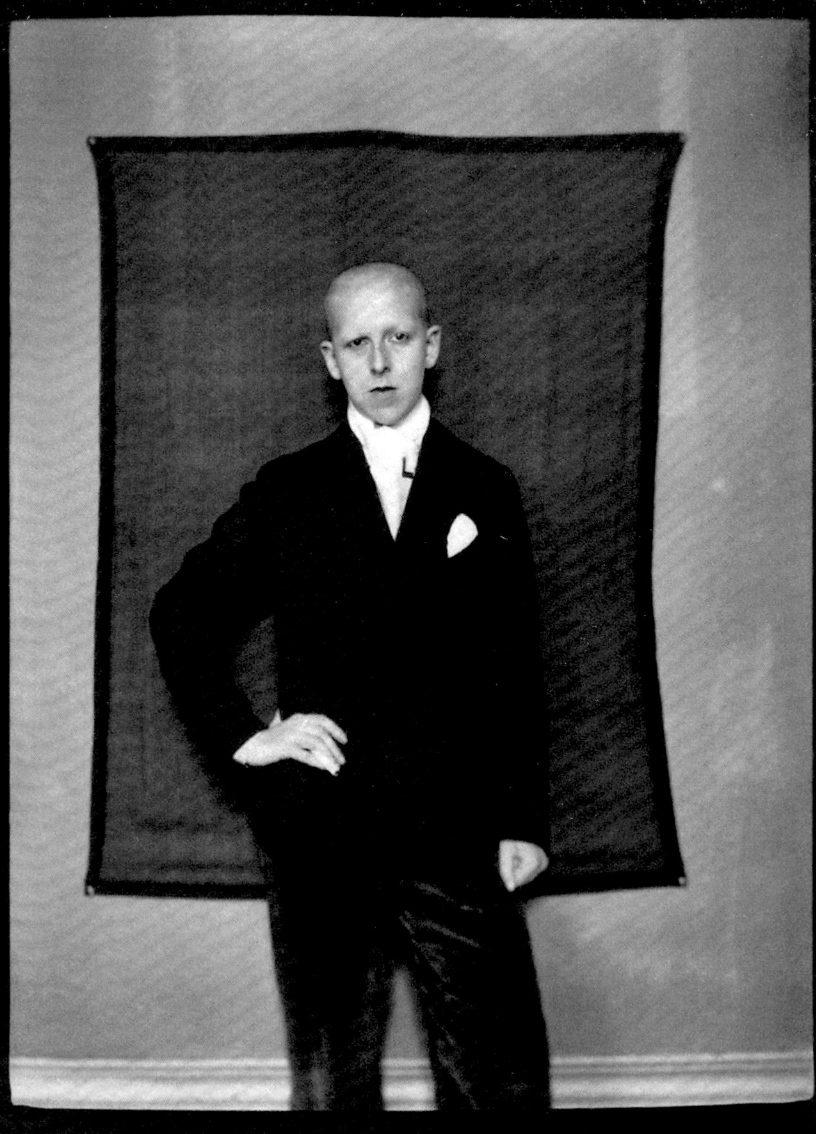

7. Le Croisic, 1921.

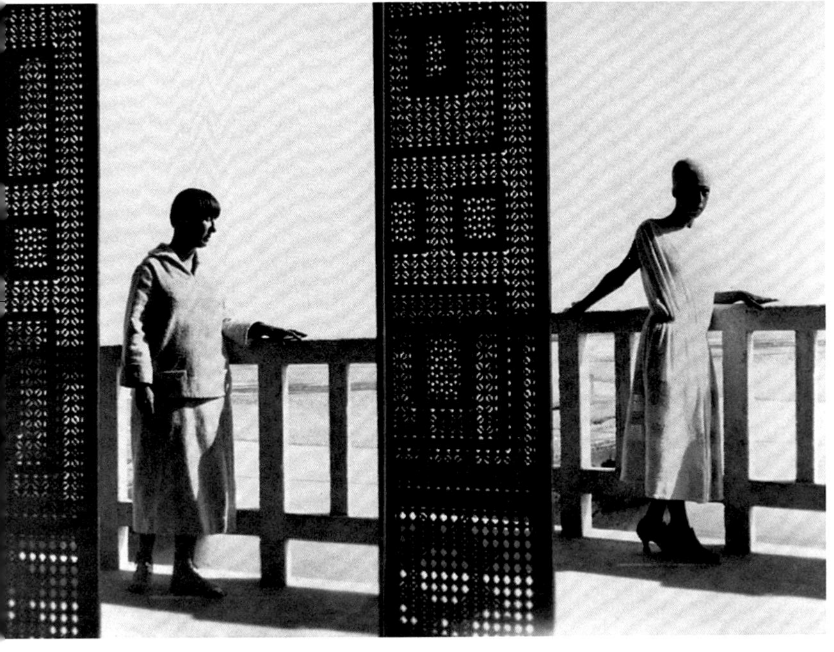

8. 1926.

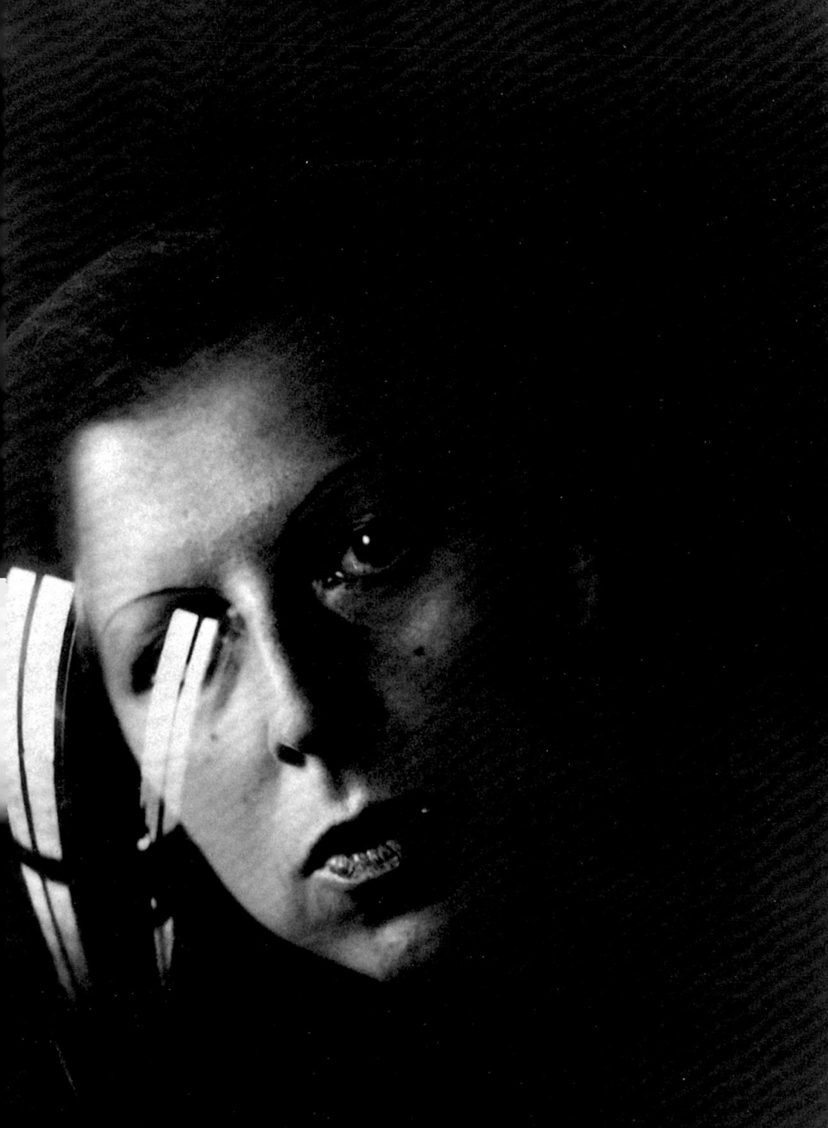

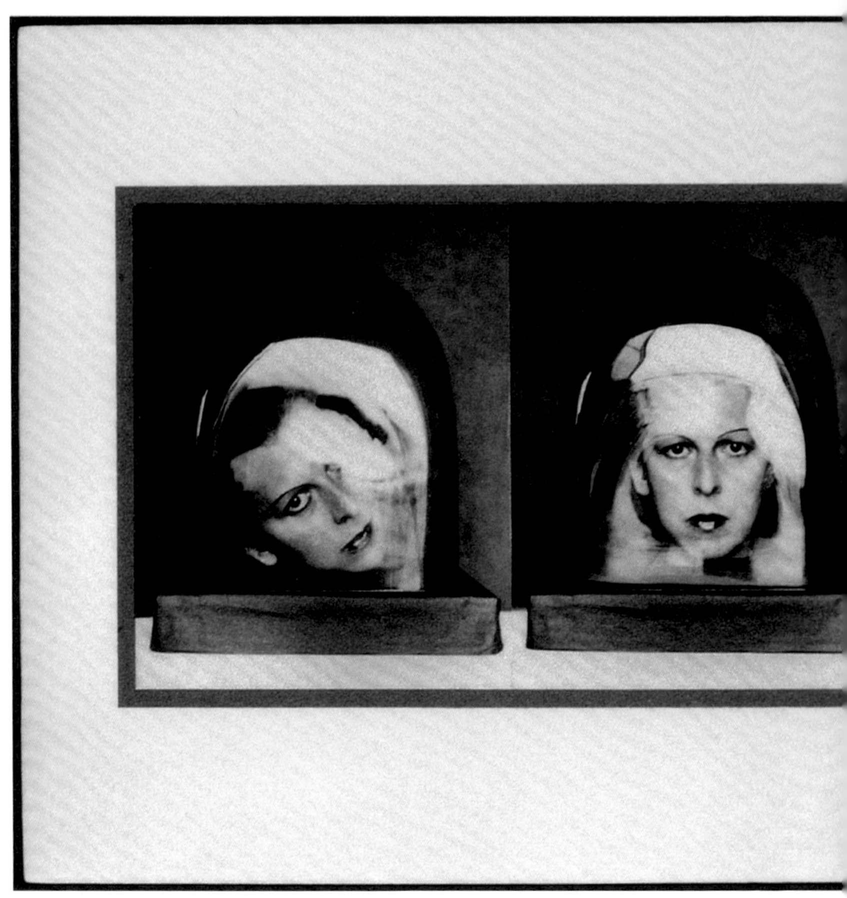

9. *Studies for a Keepsake*, 1926.

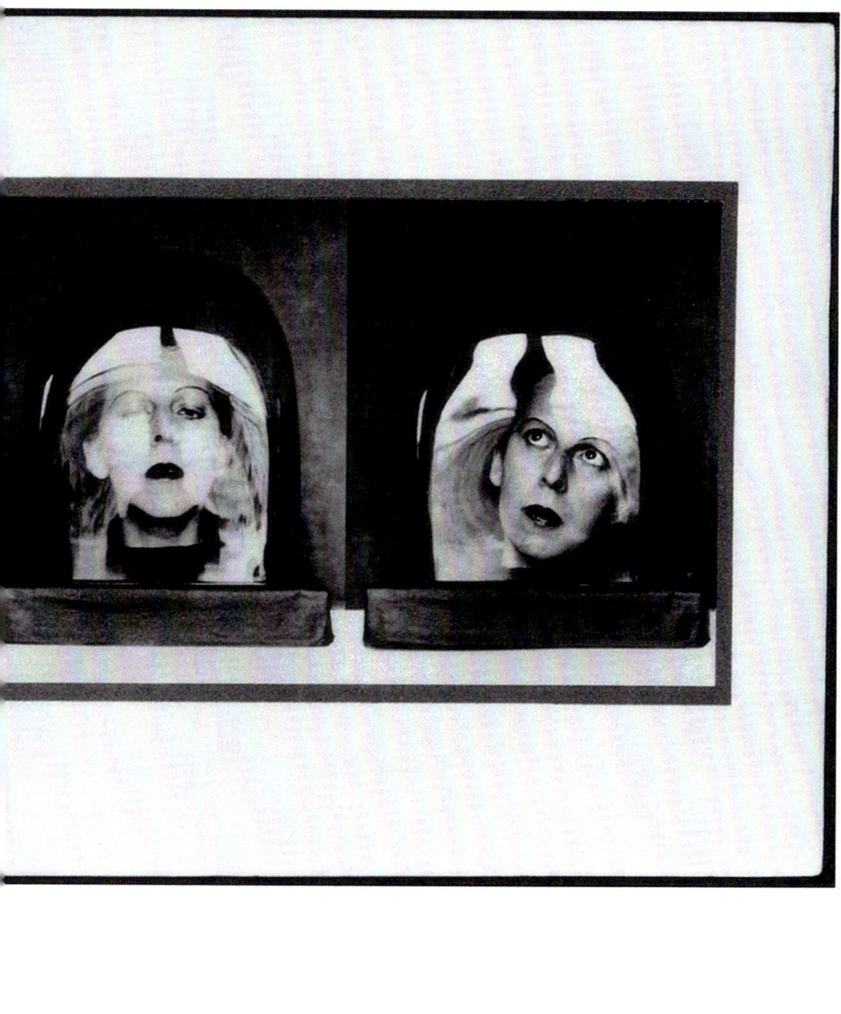

10. Portrait of Henri Michaux, 1925.

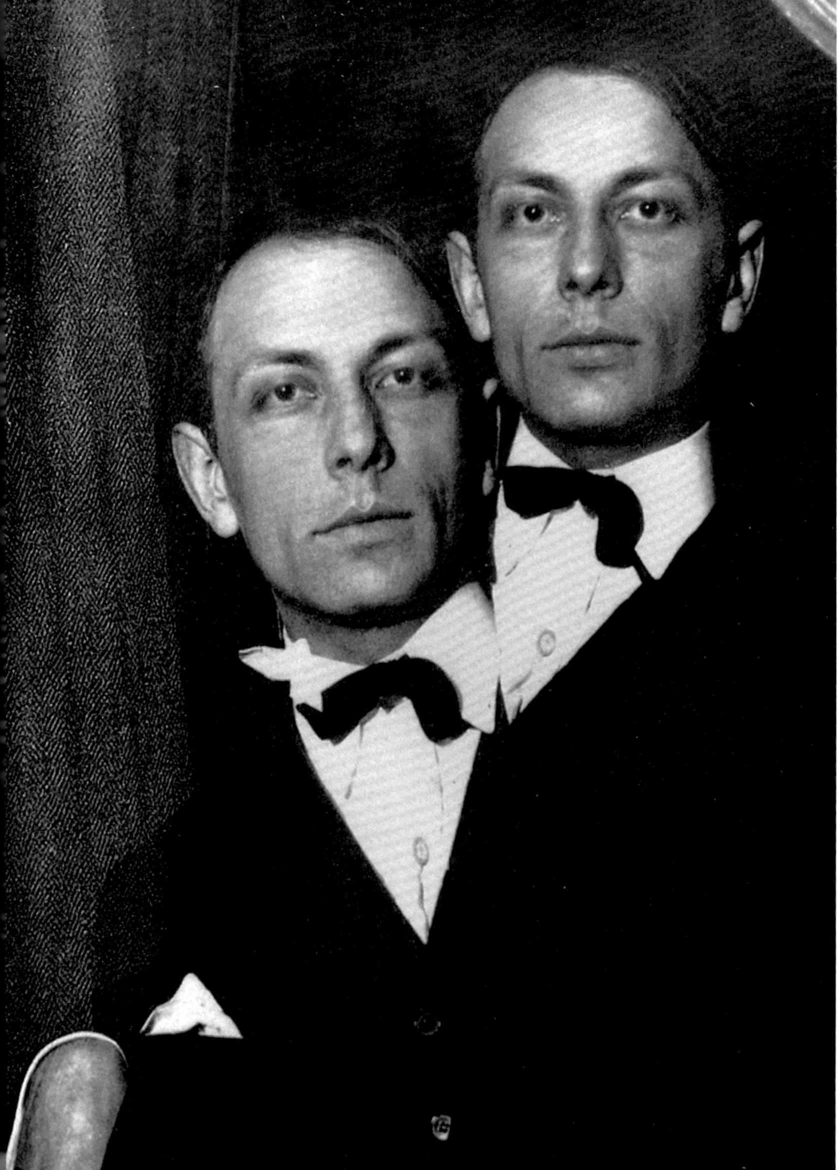

11. 1926.

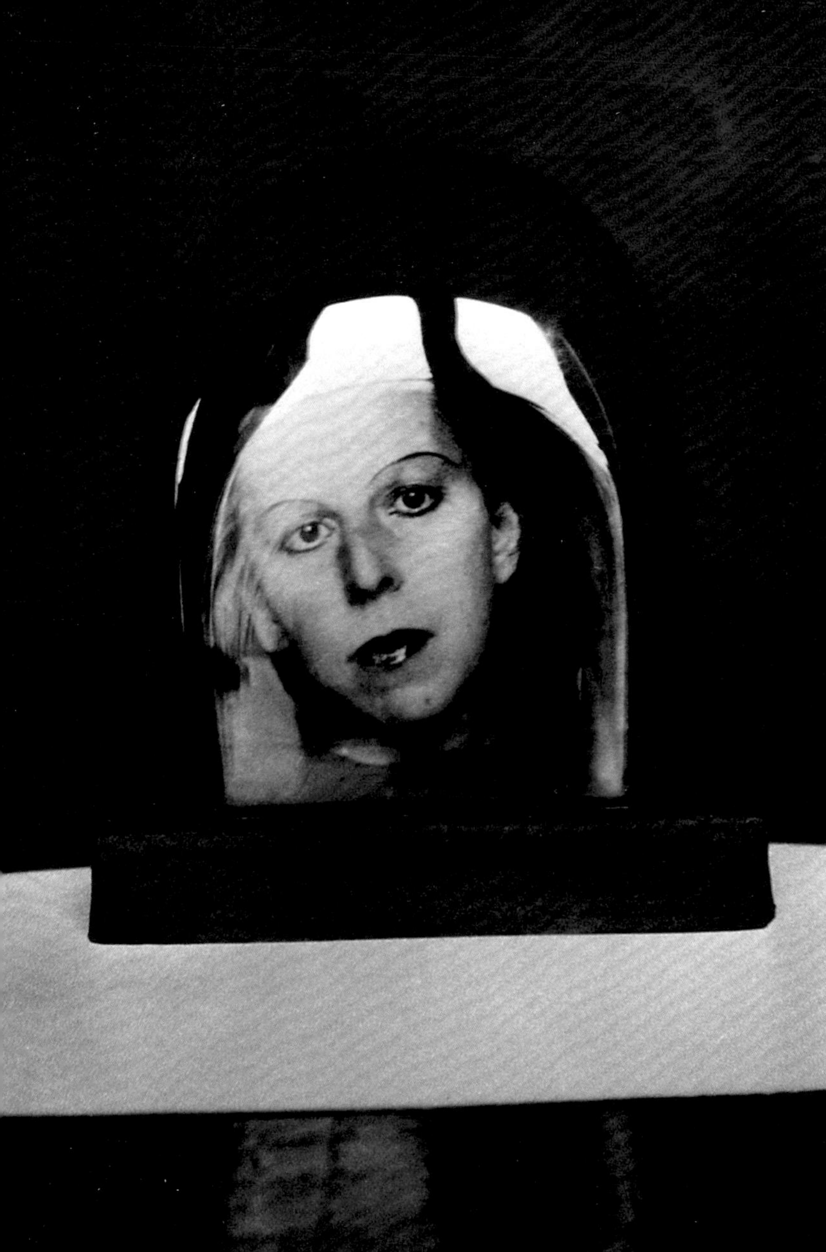

12. 1927.

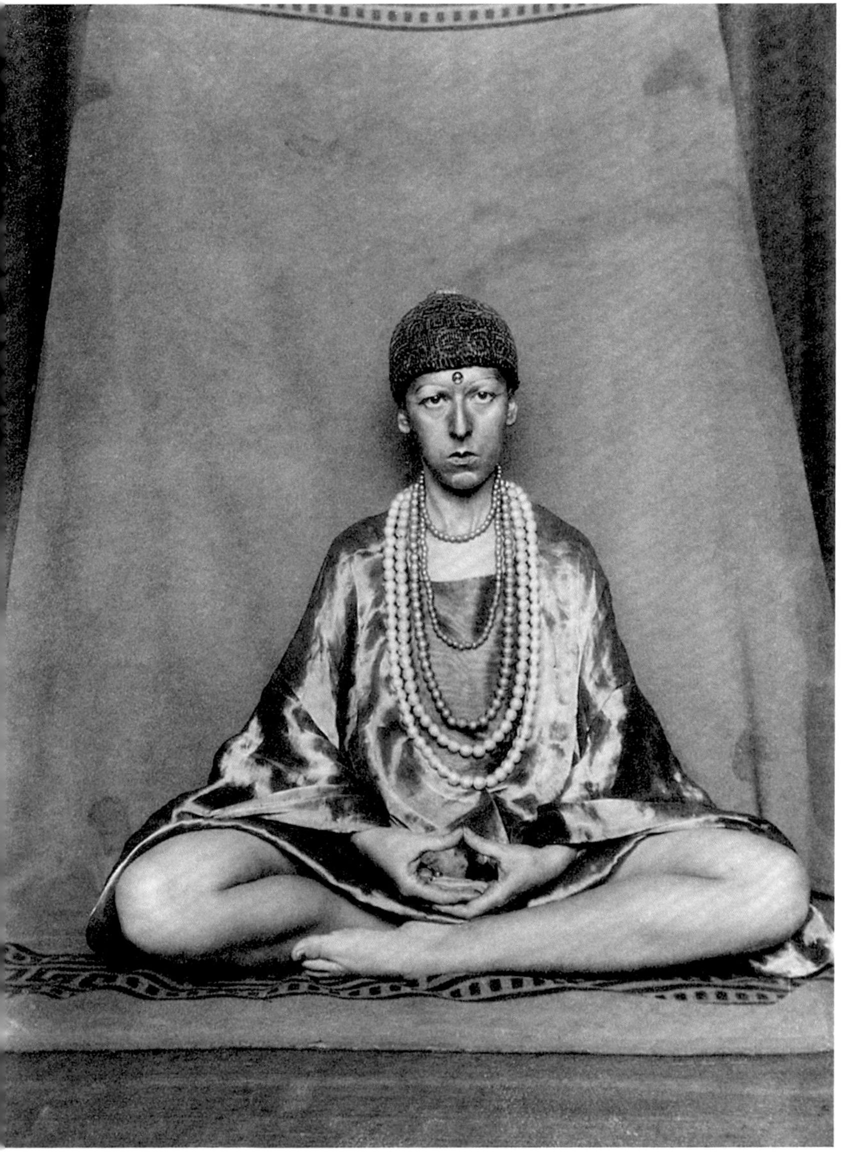

13. *Between Us*, 1926.

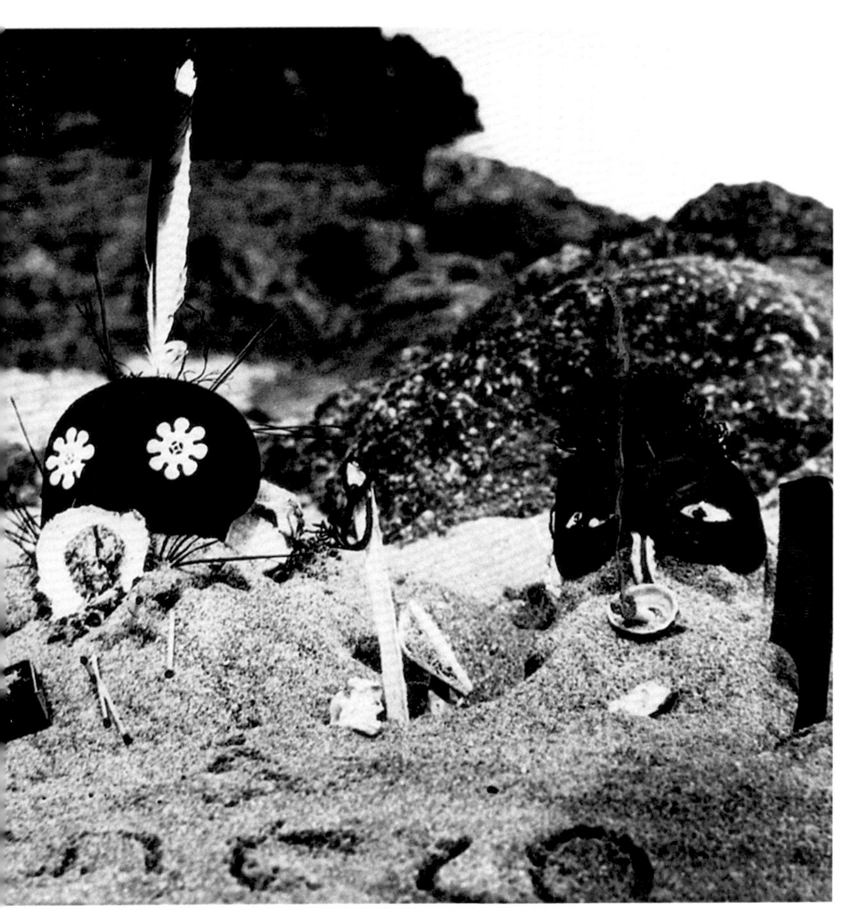

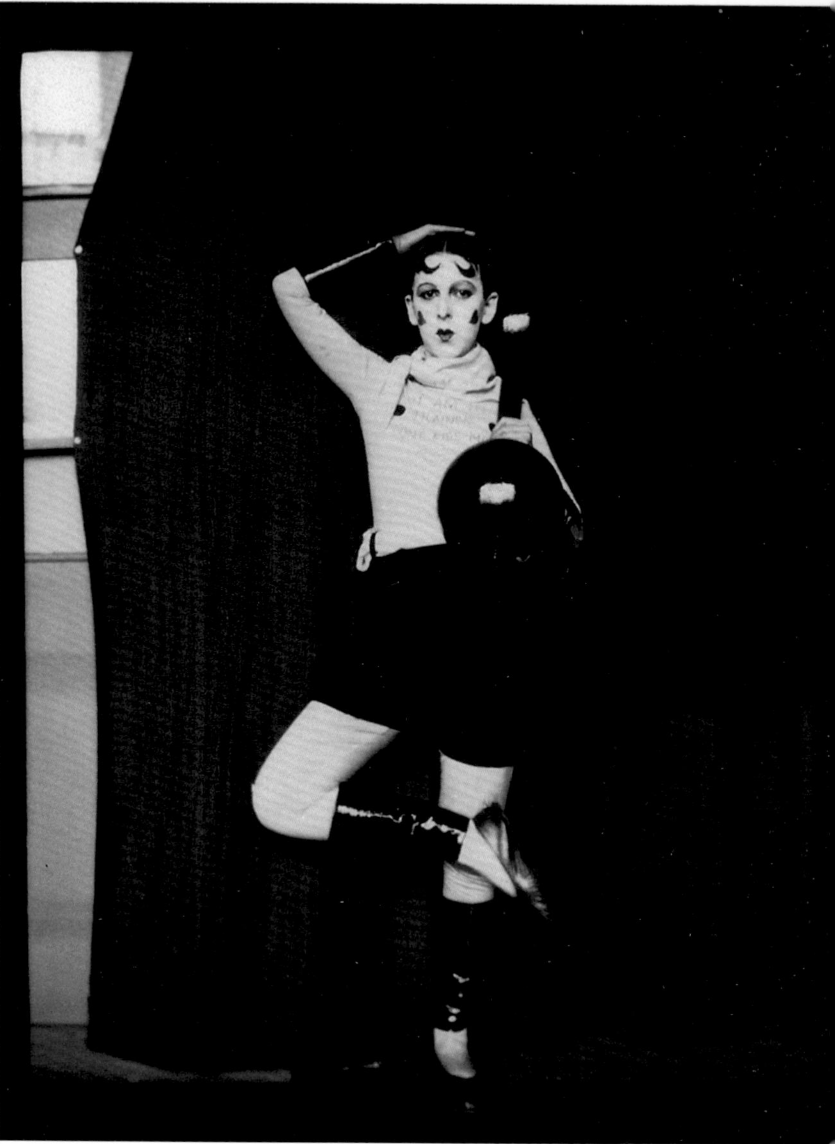

14–15. 1927.

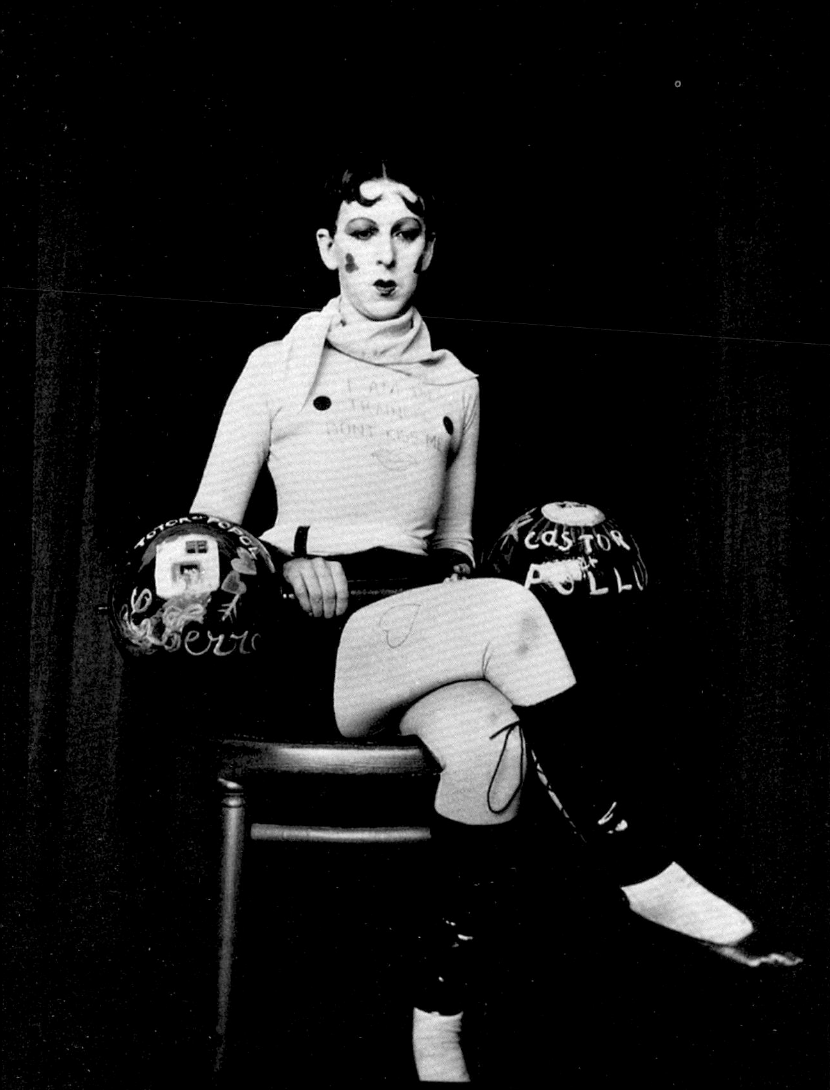
I AM IN TRAINING
DONT KISS ME
TOTOR POPOL
Liberté
CASTOR et POLLU

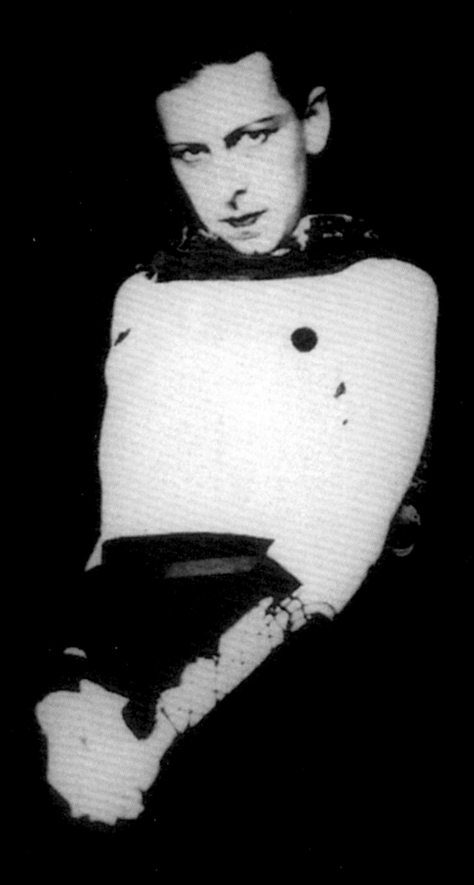

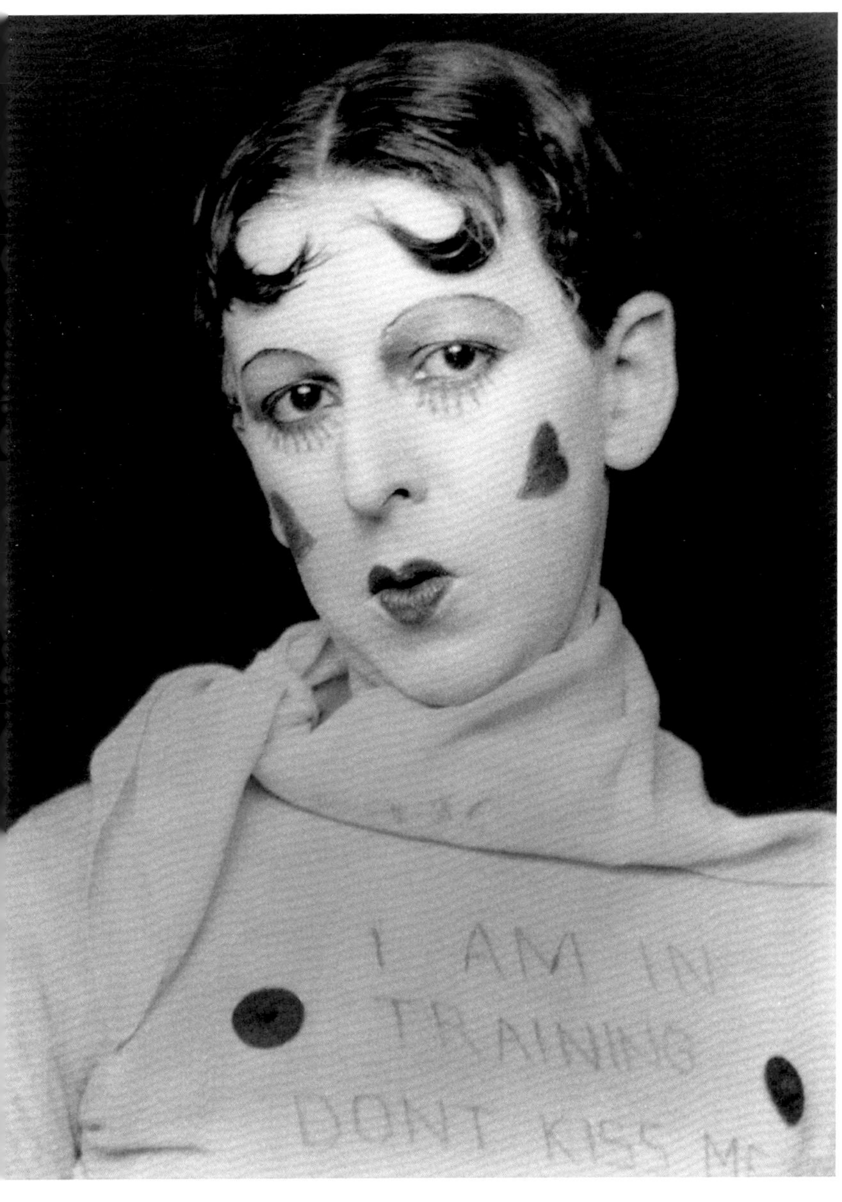

16. c. 1927.

17. 1927.

18. c. 1927.

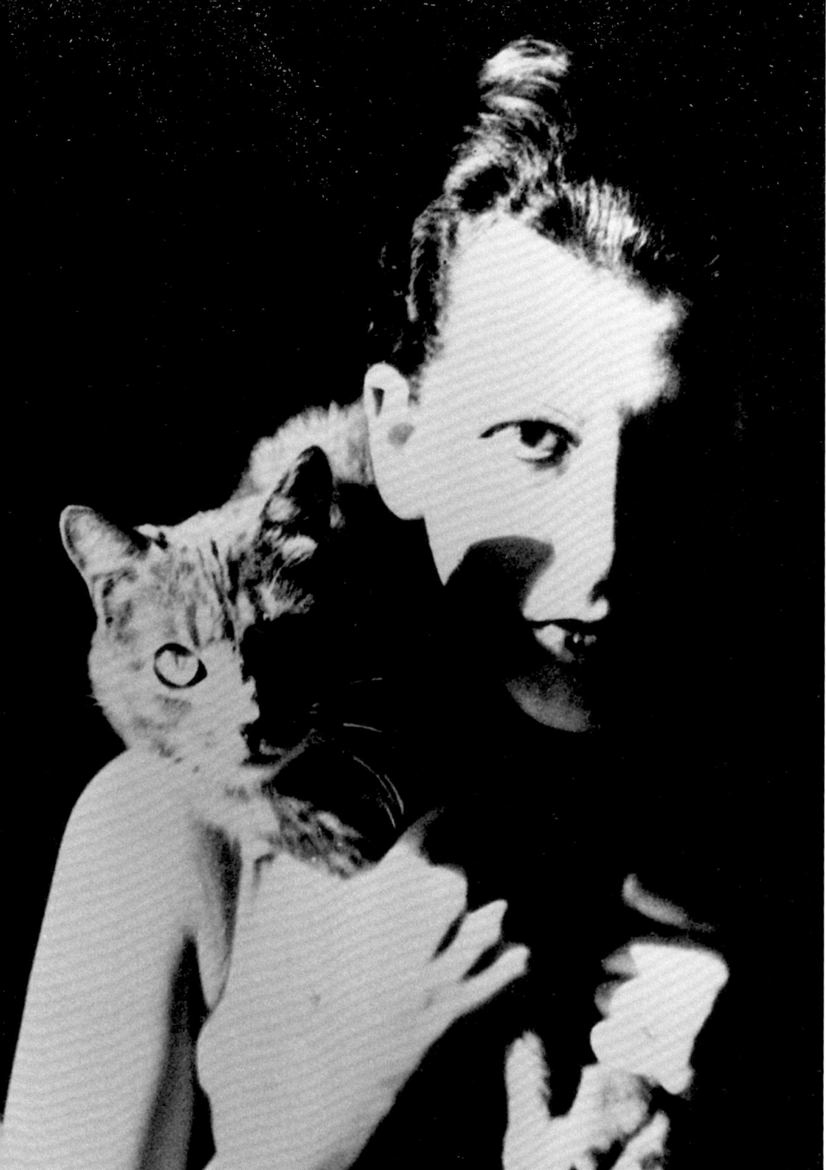

19. c. 1927.

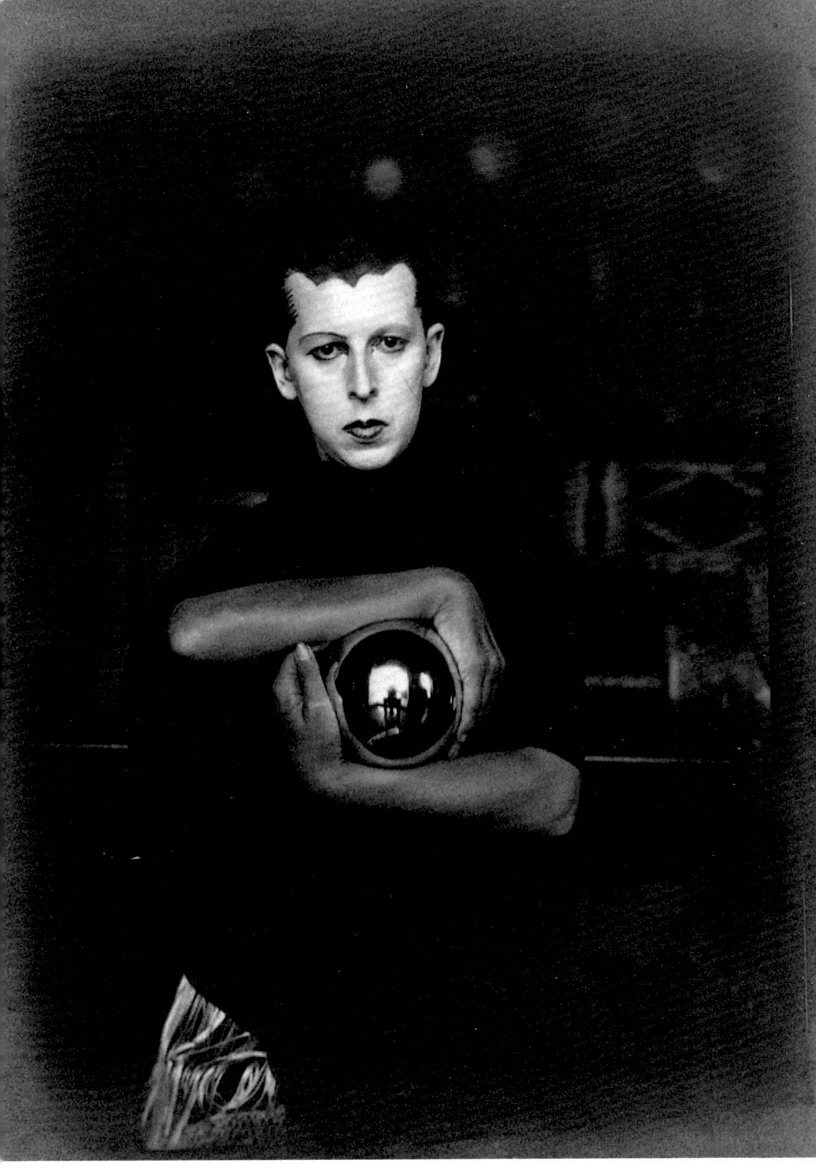

20. c. 1927.

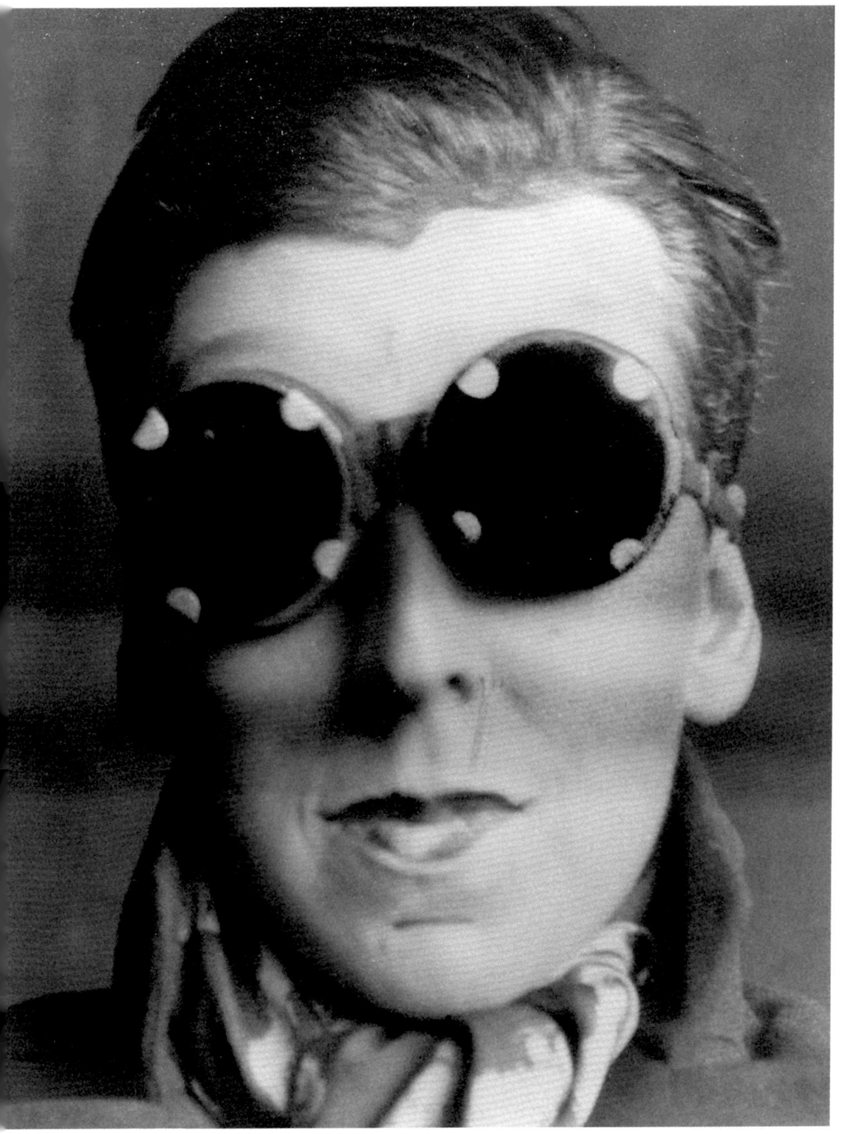

21. c. 1928.

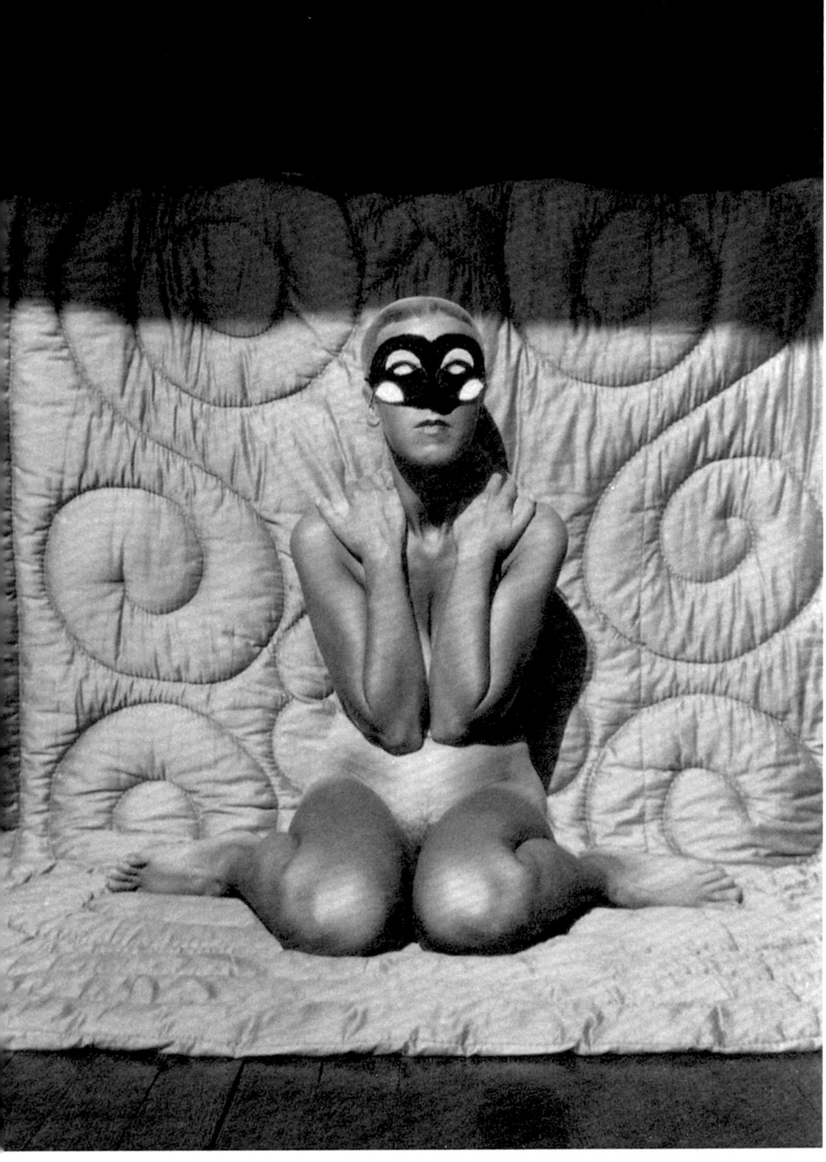

22. c. 1928.

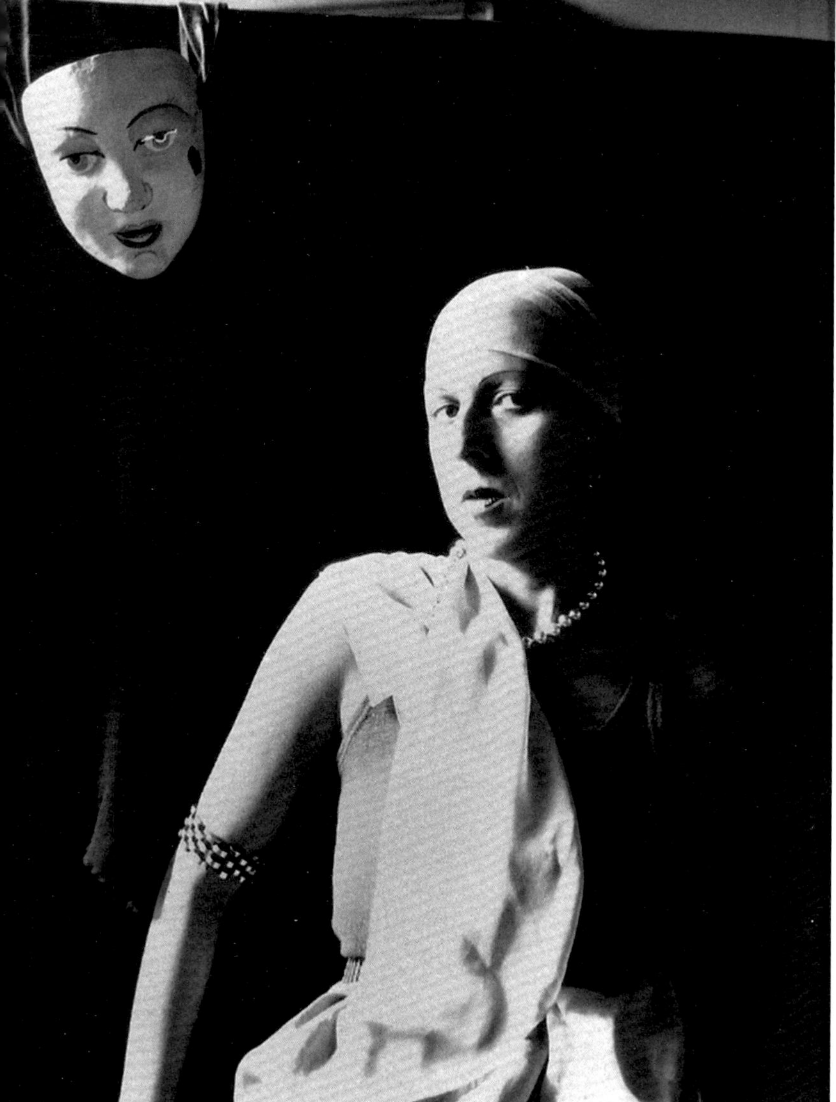

23. 1928.

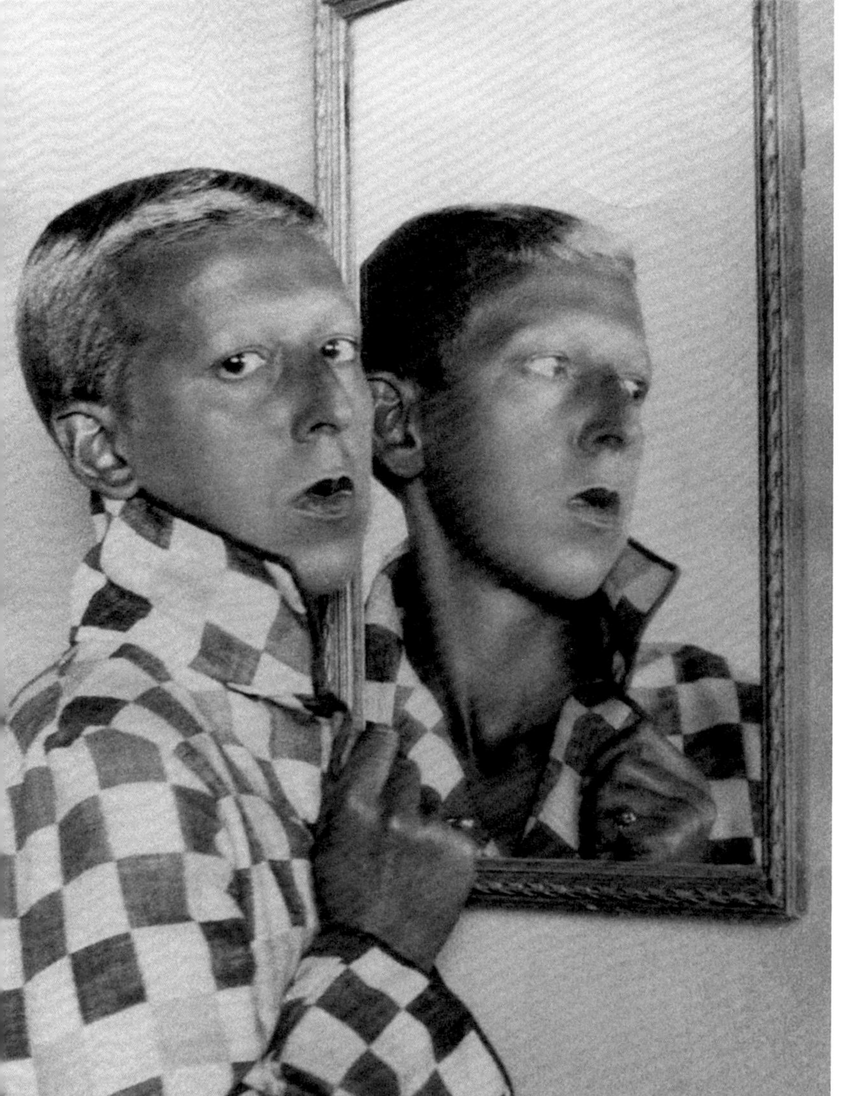

24. c. 1928.

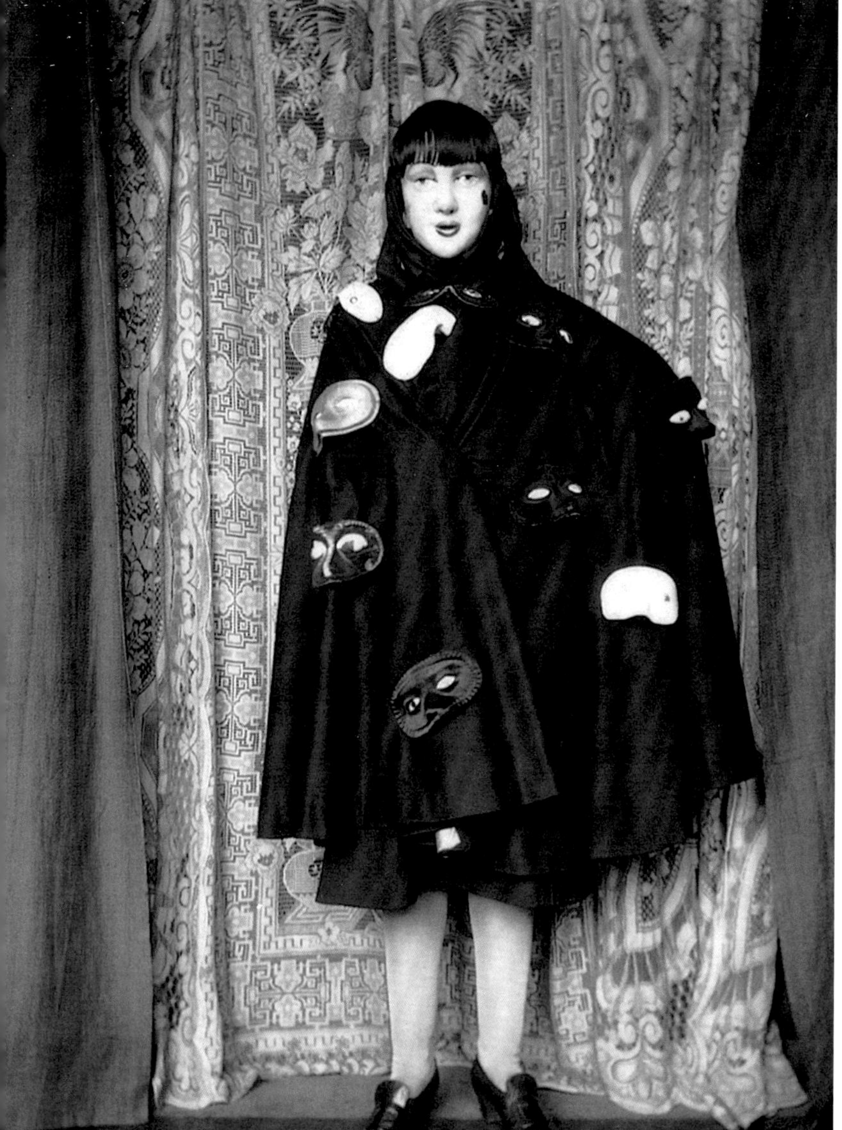

25. *What Do You Want From Me?*, 1928.

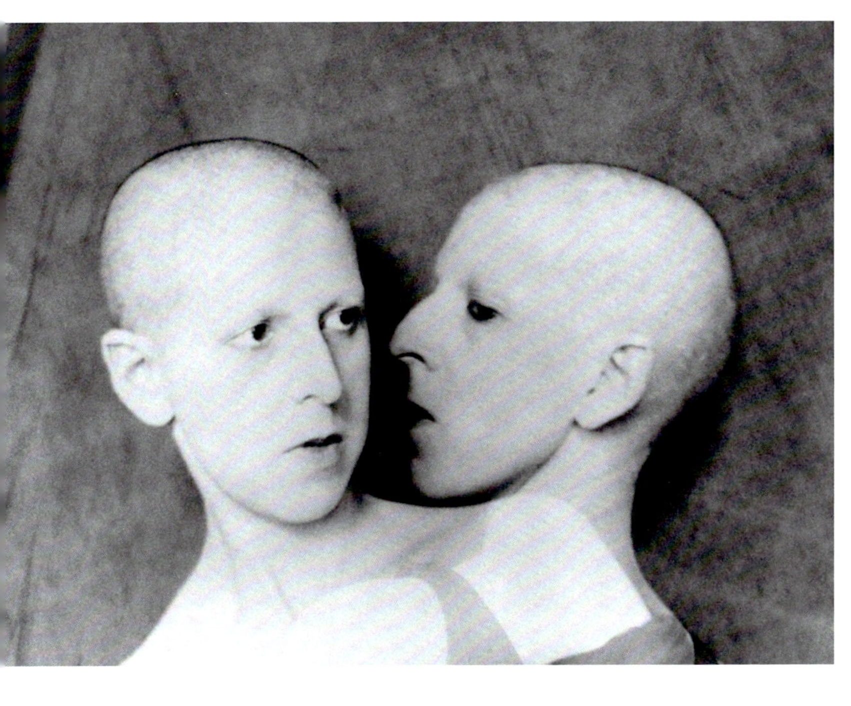

26. c. 1928.

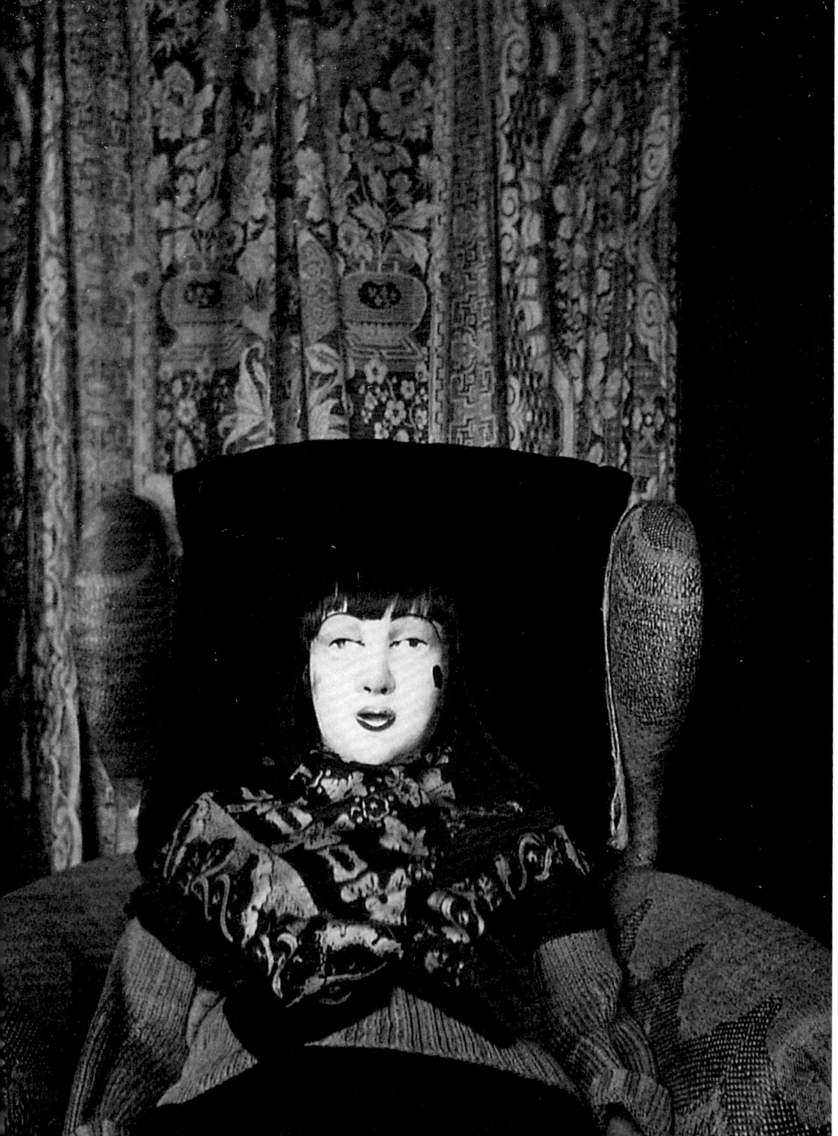

27. 1929.

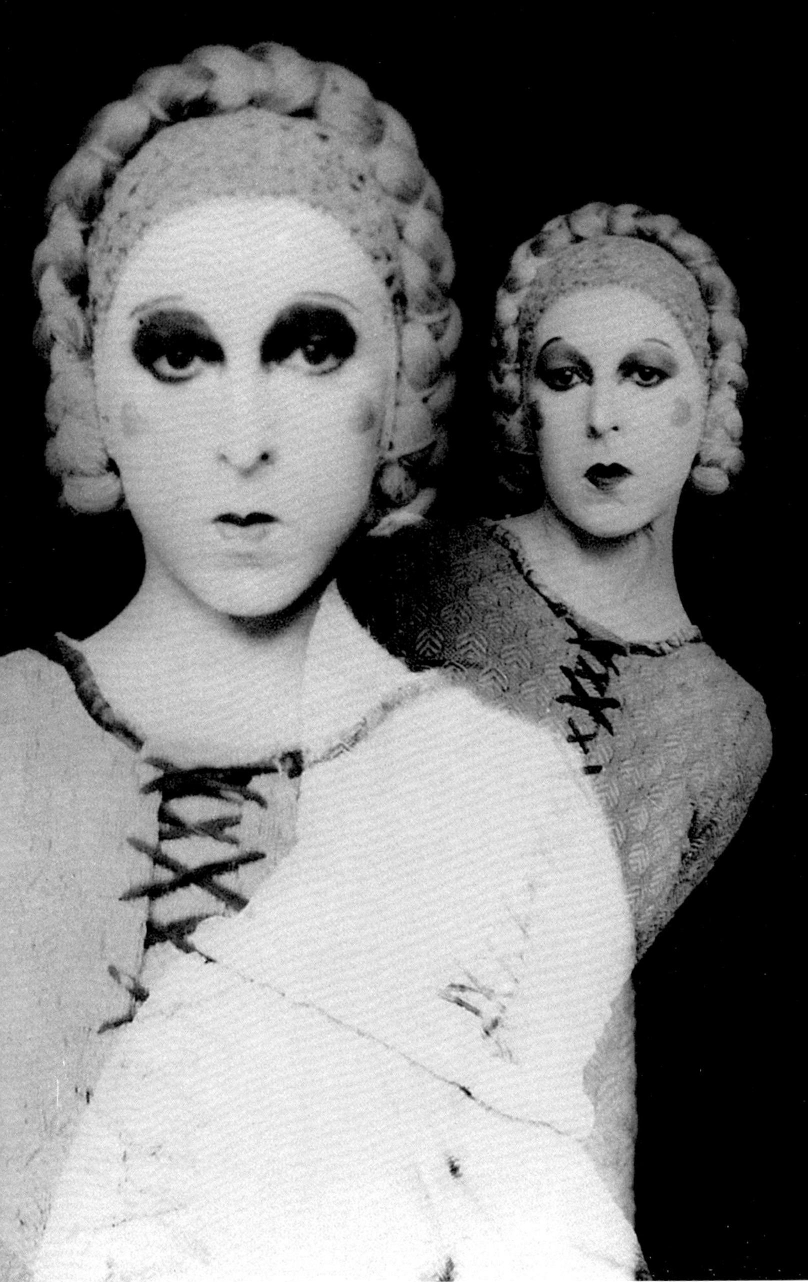

28. c. 1928.

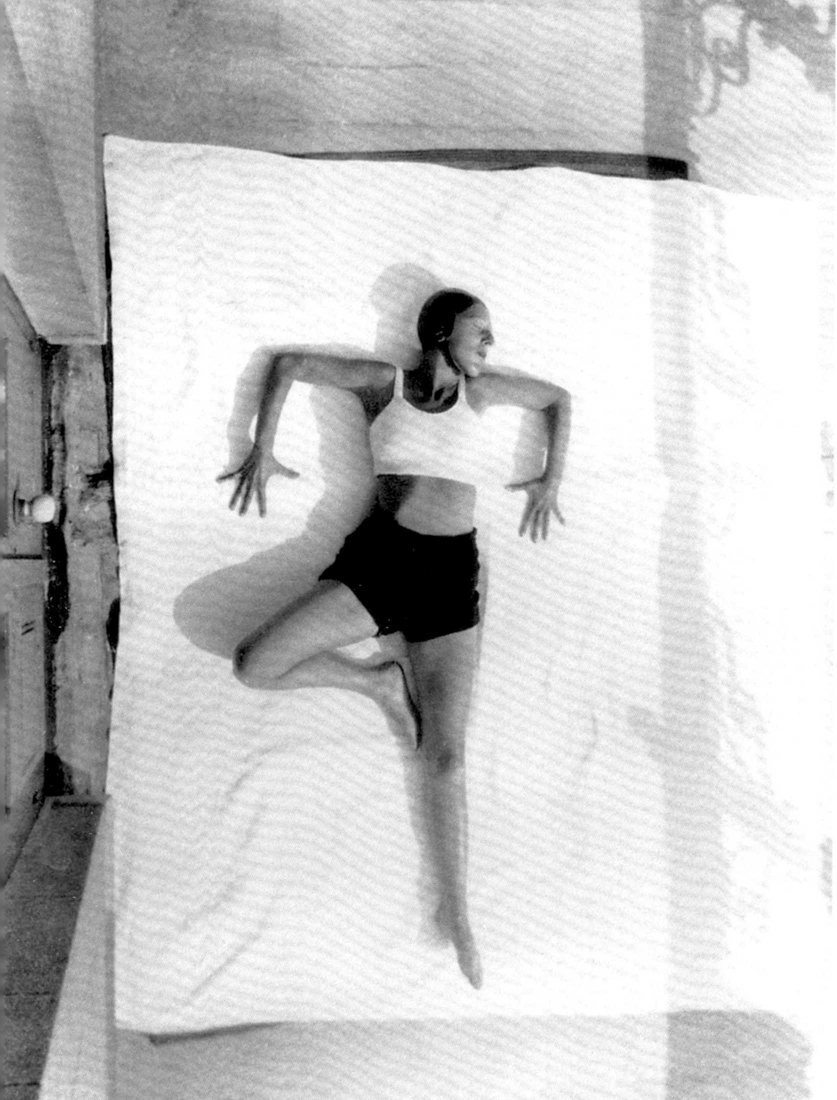

29. 1929.

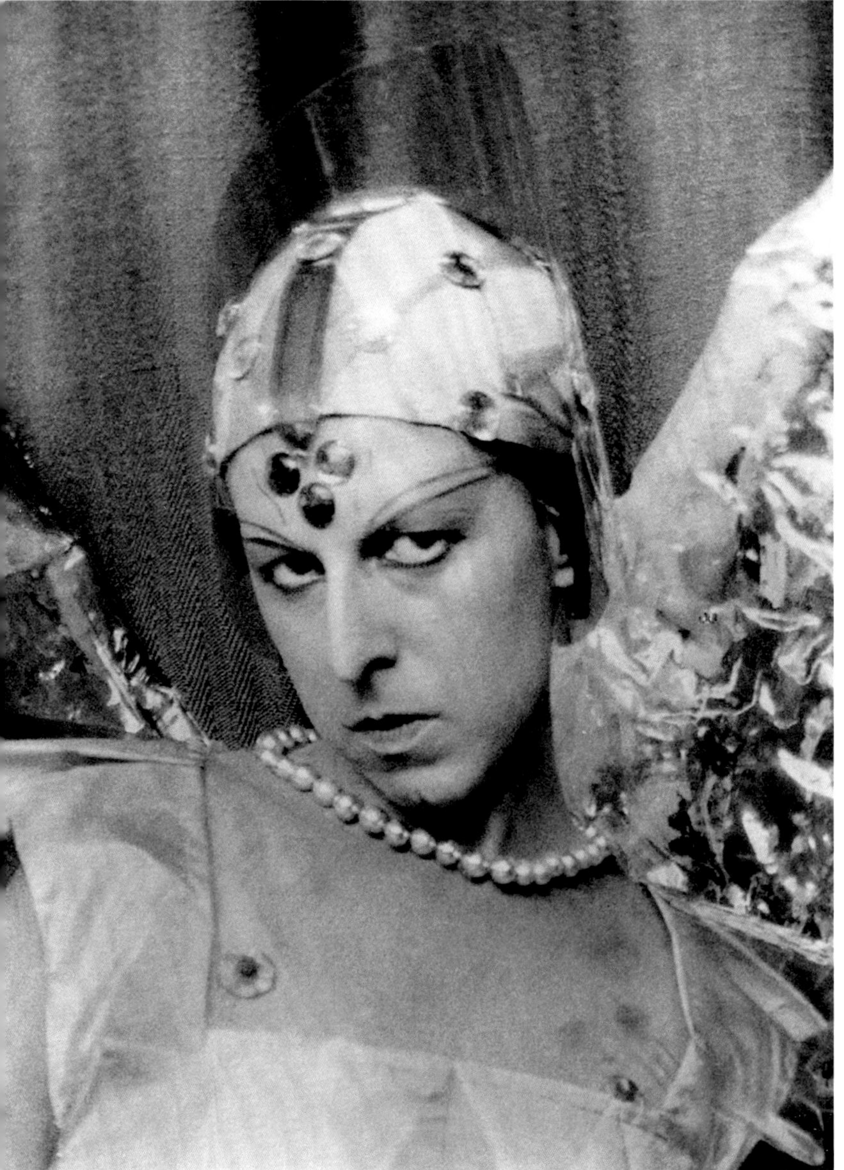

30. c. 1928.

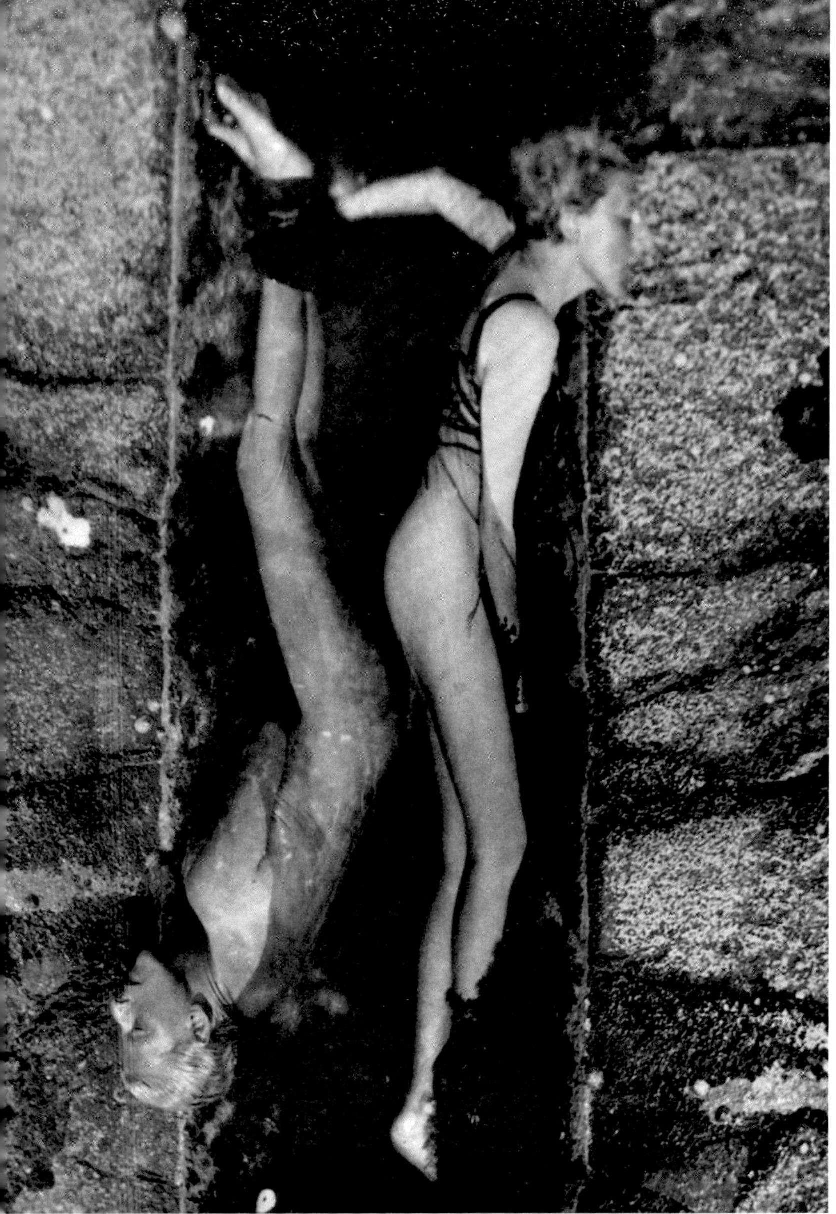

31. c. 1928.

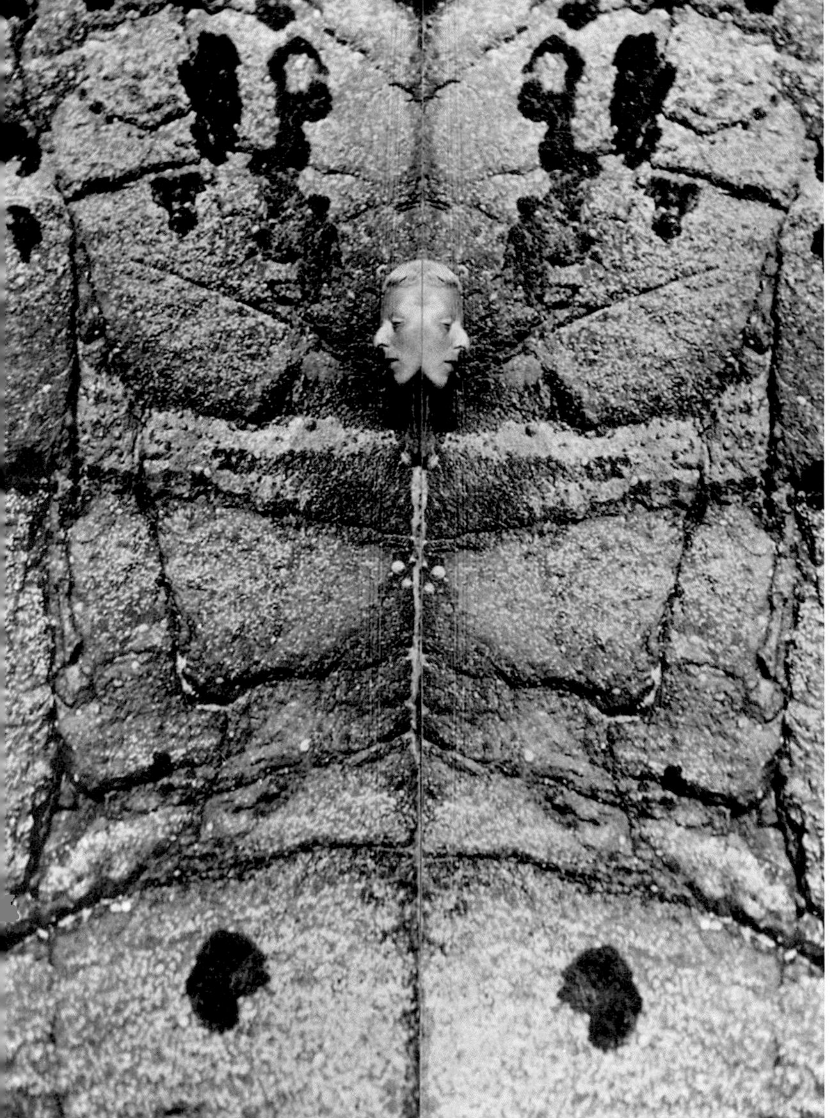

32. c. 1929. Published in *Bifur*, no. 5, 1930.

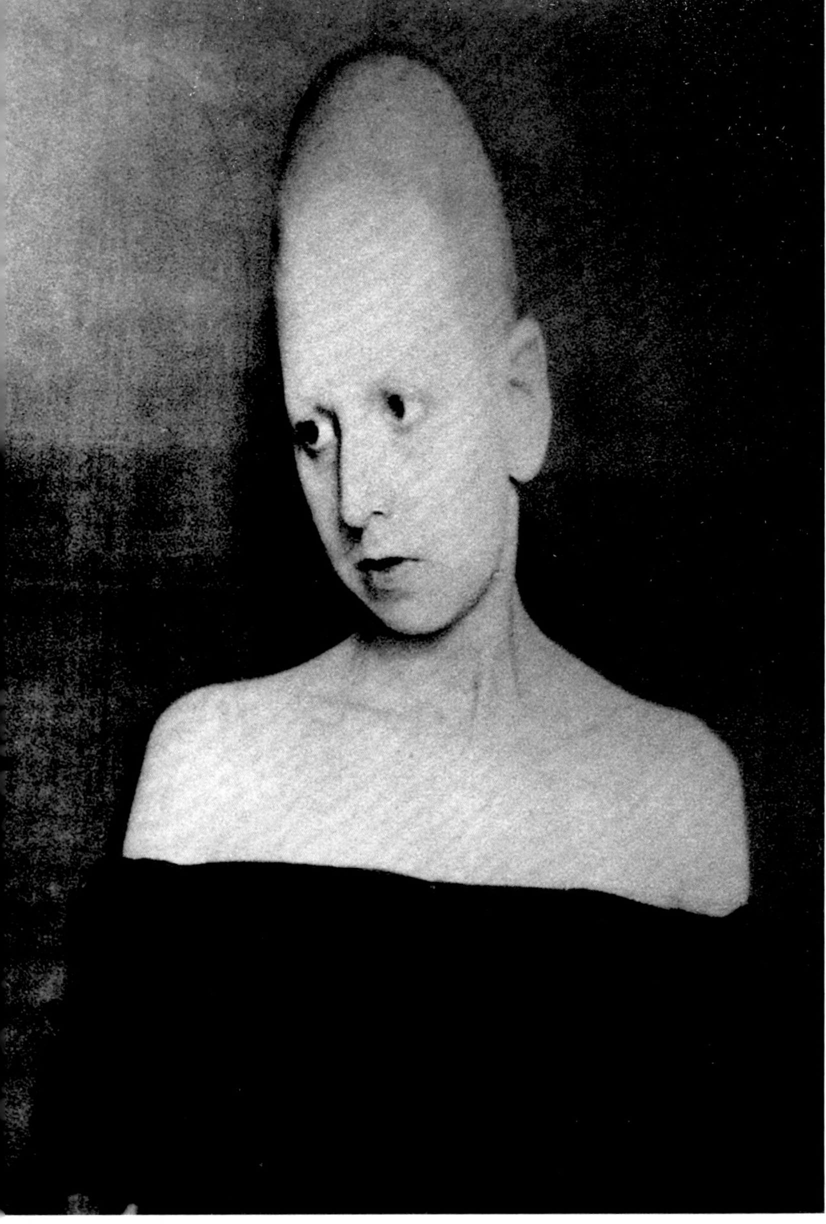

33. 1929–1930.

Plate III from *Aveux non avenus*,
Éditions du Carrefour, Paris, 1930.

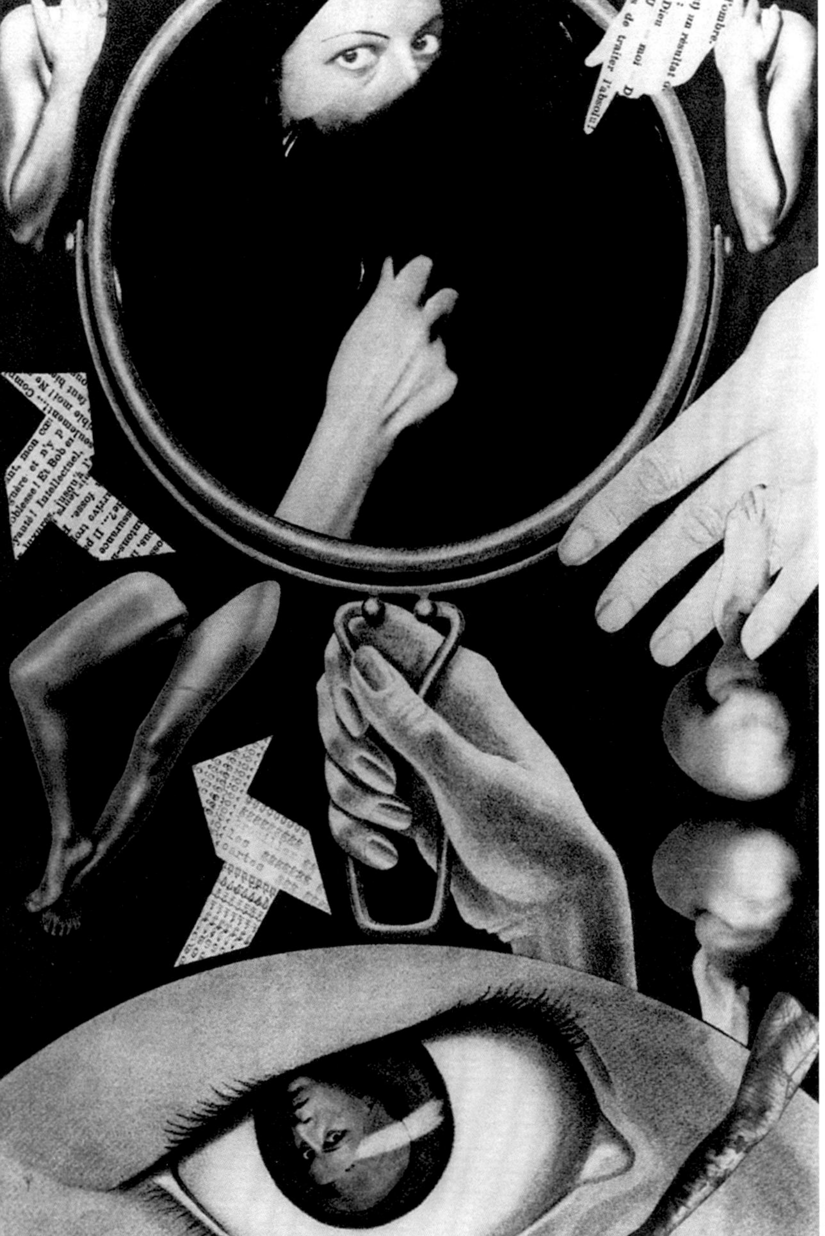

34. 1929–1930.

Plate V in *Aveux non avenus*,

Éditions du Carrefour, Paris, 1930.

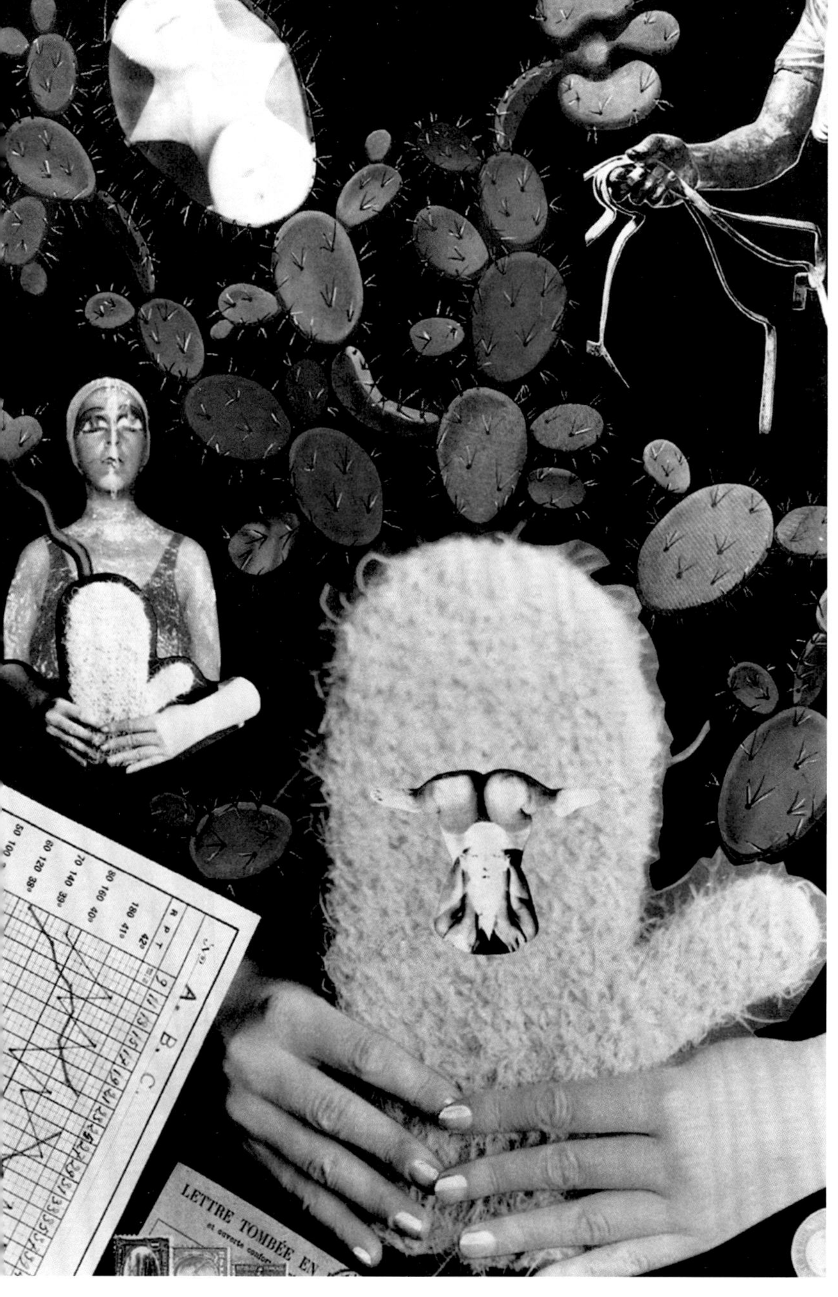
RPT
50 100
60 120 38°
70 140 39°
80 160 40°
180 41°
42°
A . B . C .
LETTRE TOMBÉE EN

35. 1929–1930.

Plate VIII in *Aveux non avenus*,

Éditions du Carrefour, Paris, 1930.

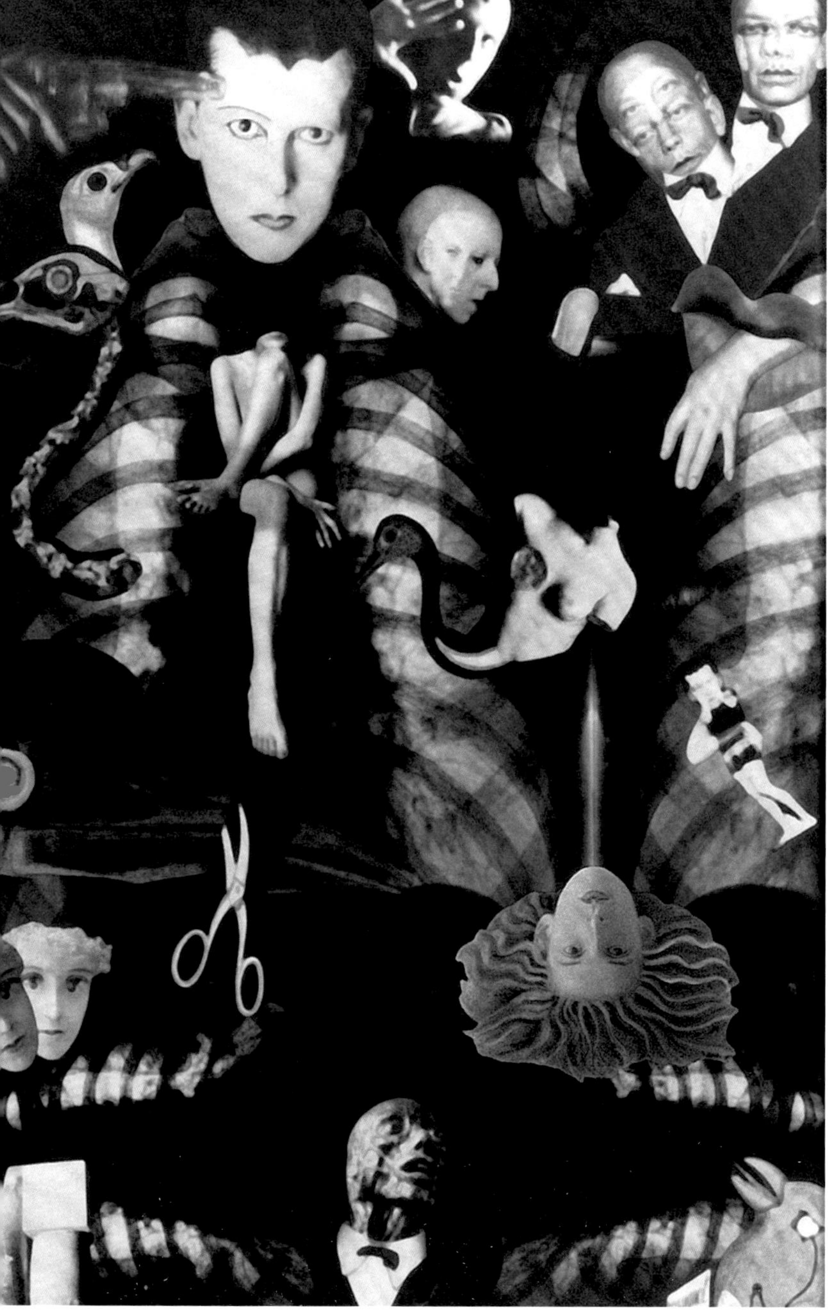

36. 1929–1930.

Plate X in *Aveux non avenus*,
Éditions du Carrefour, Paris, 1930.

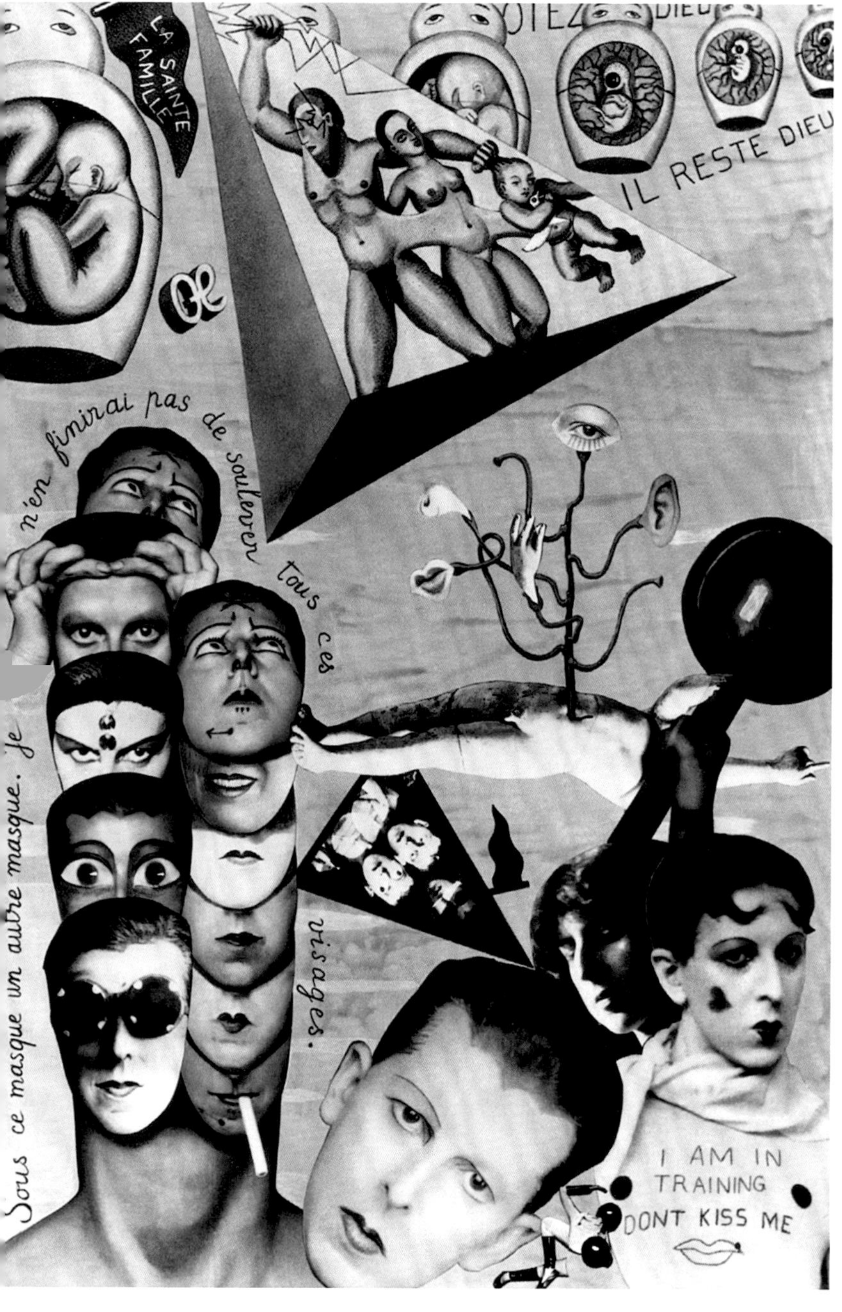

LA SAINTE FAMILLE
OR
ÔTEZ DIEU
IL RESTE DIEU
Sous ce masque un autre masque. Je n'en finirai pas de soulever tous ces visages.
I AM IN TRAINING
DONT KISS ME

37. c. 1930.

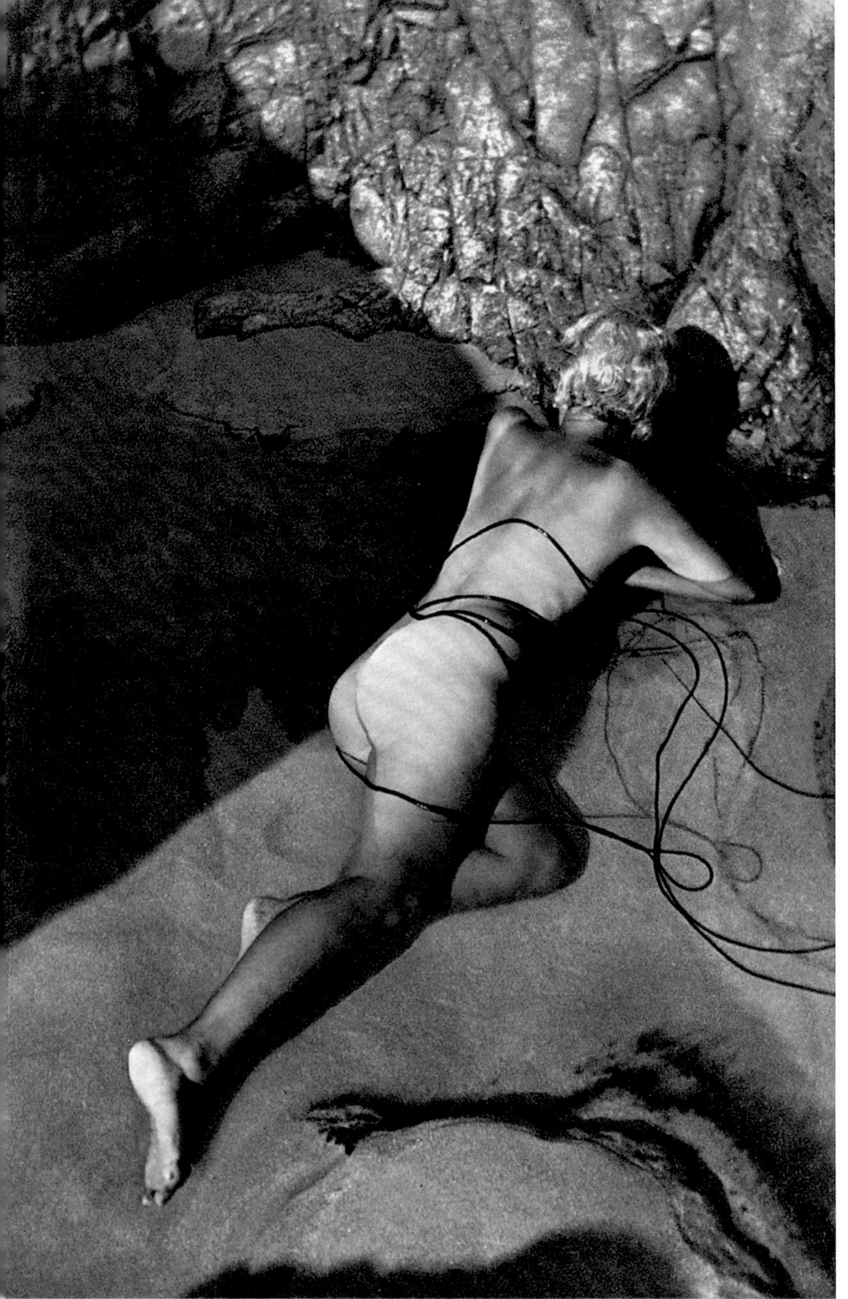

38. Portrait of Robert Desnos, 1930.

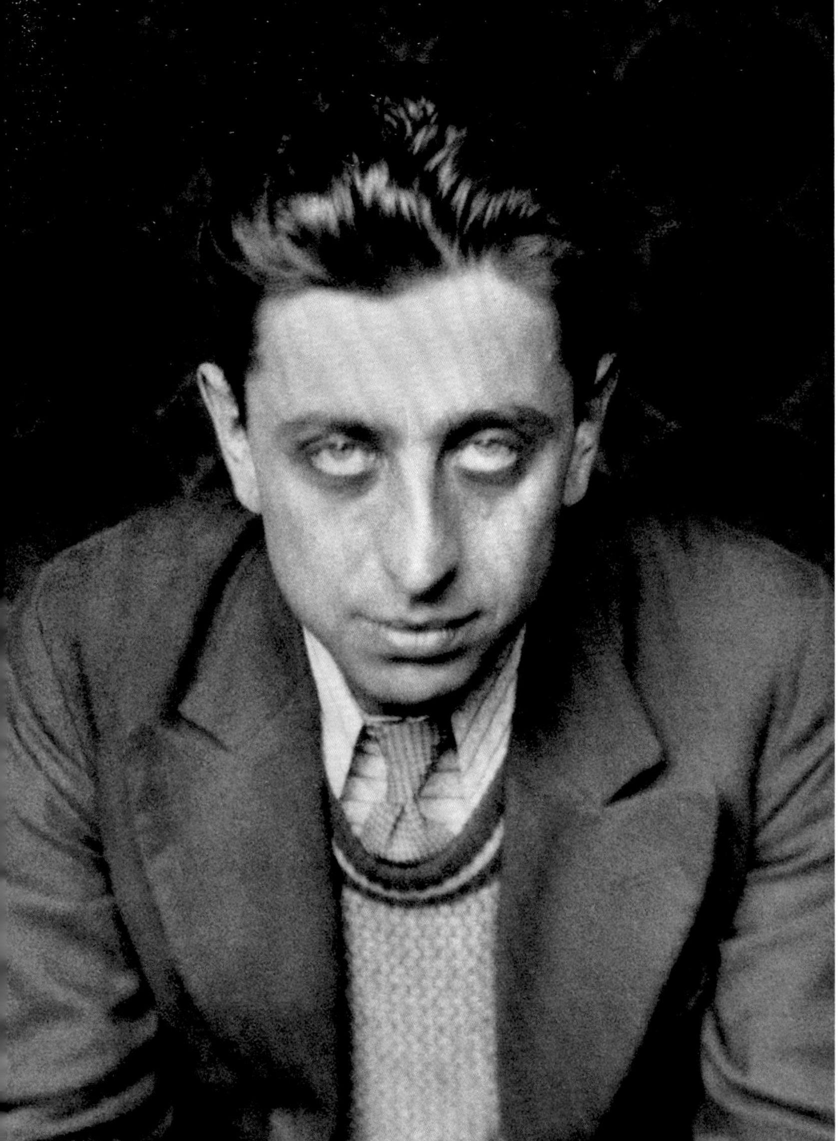

39. *Battle of Stones*, 1931.

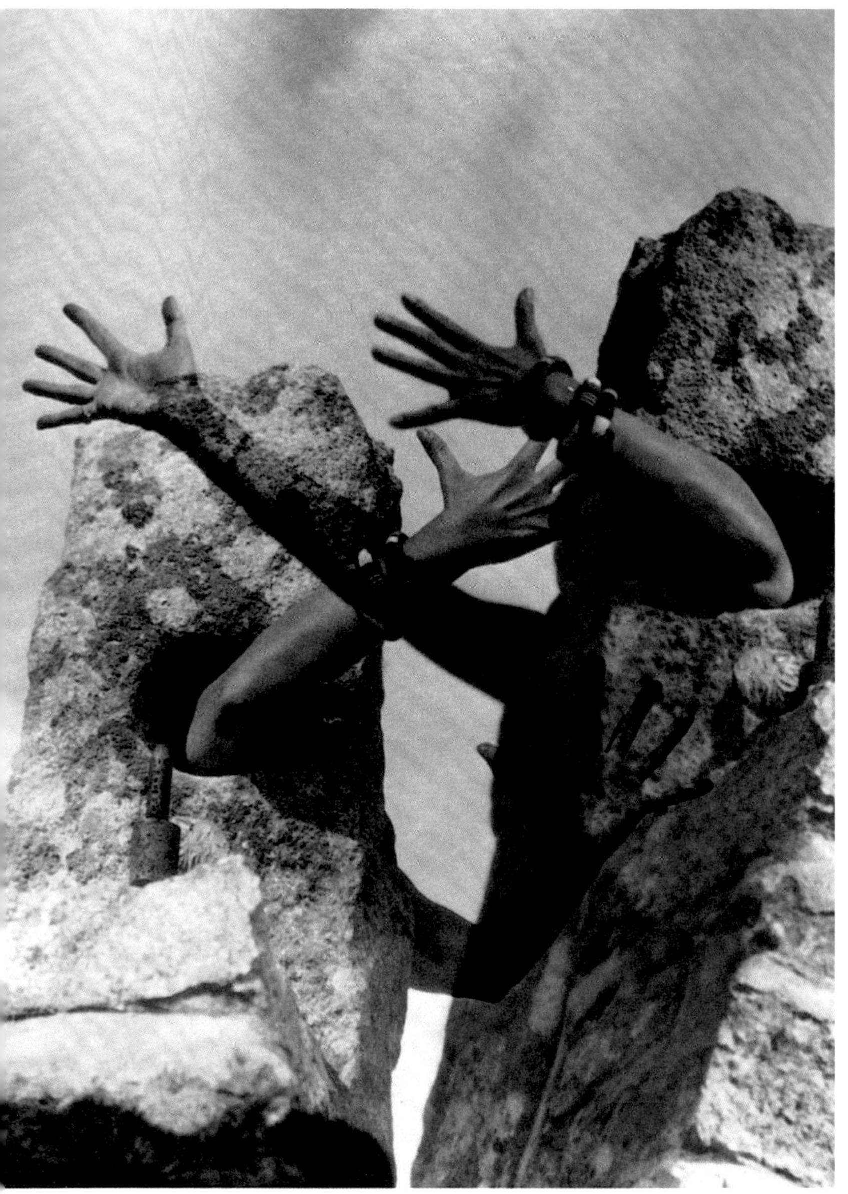

40. *The Father*, 1932.

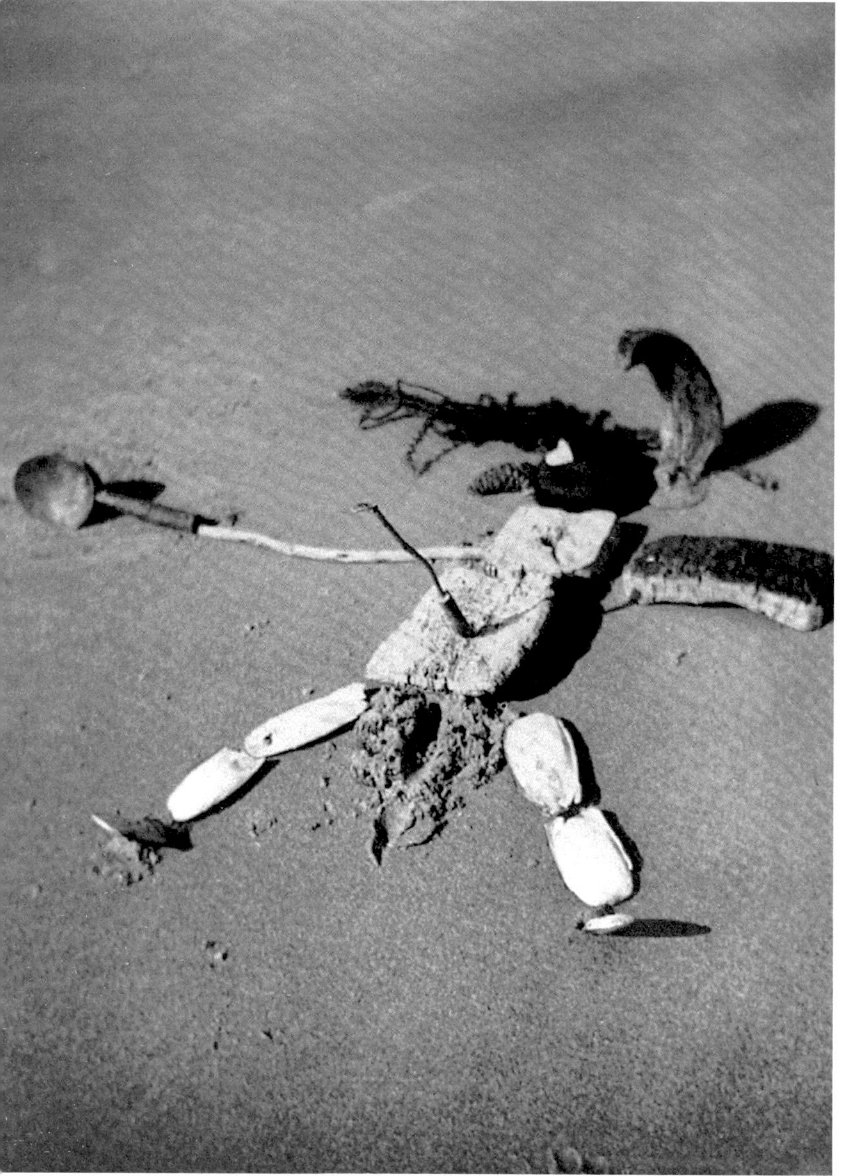

41. 1932.

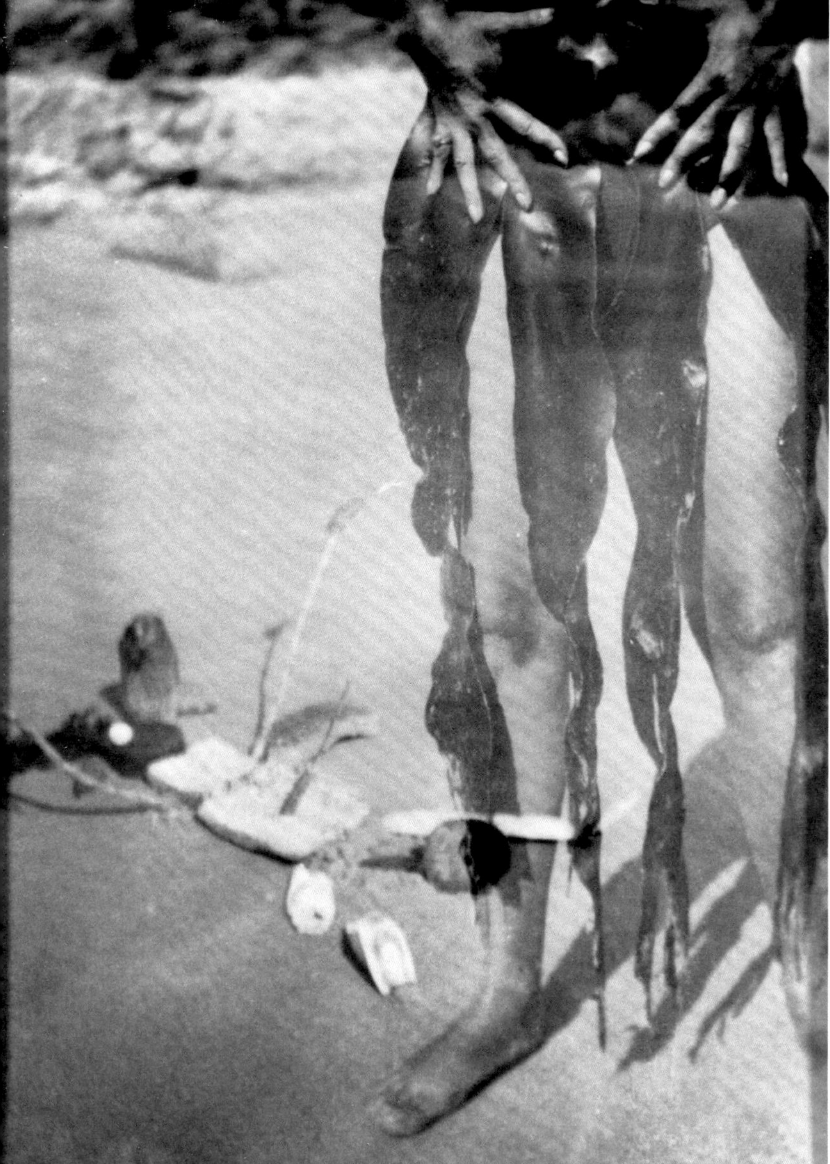

42.1932.

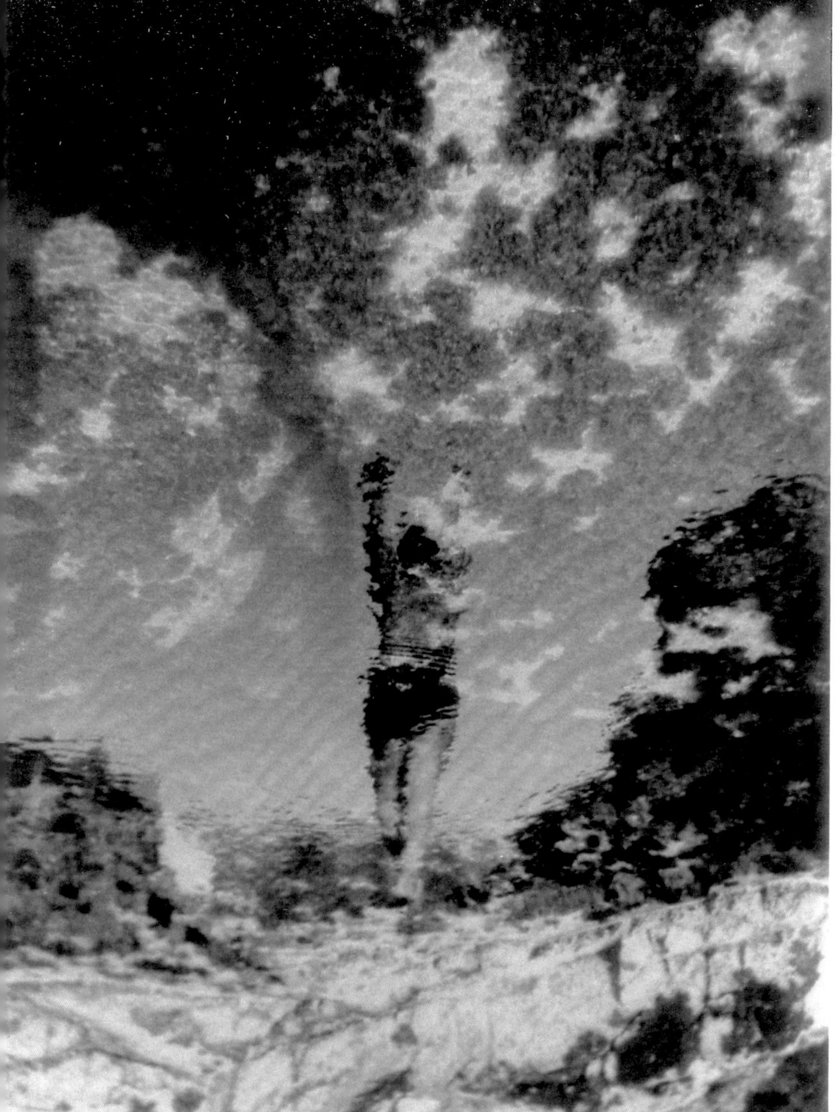

43. c. 1932.

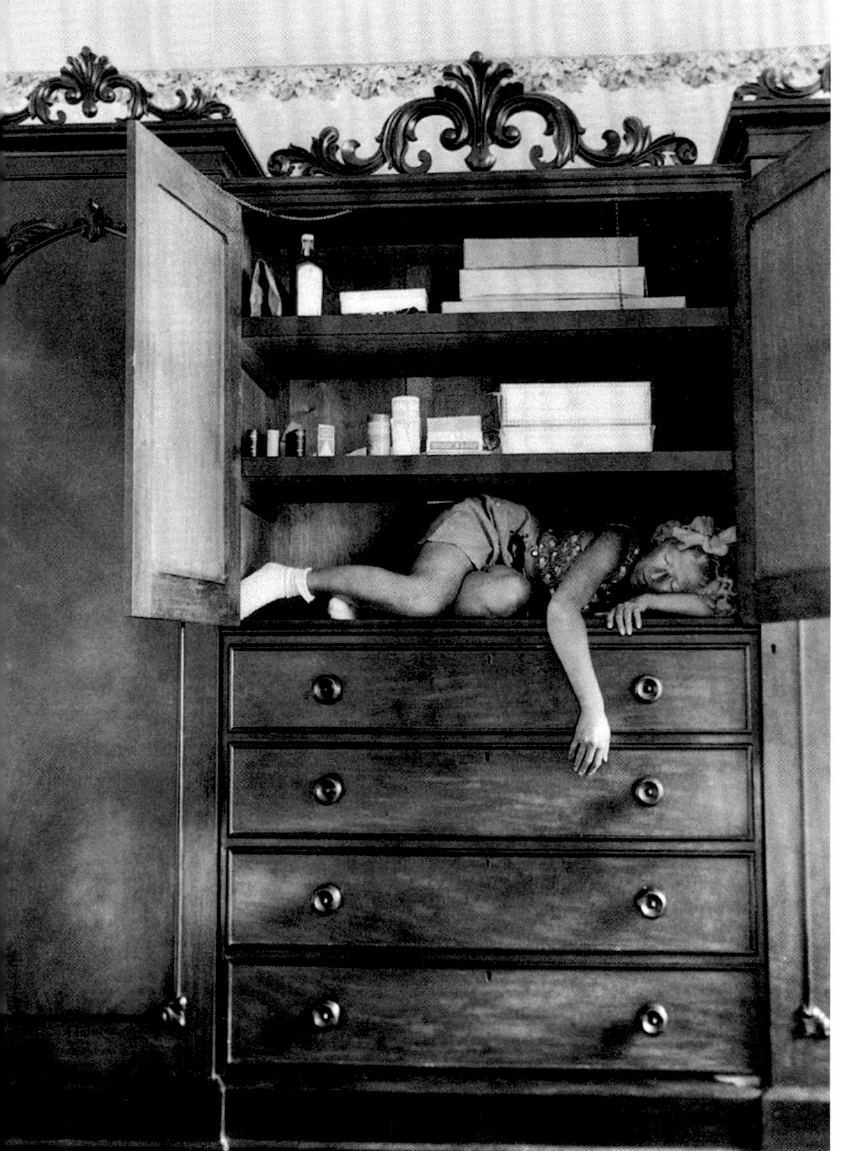

44. c. 1935.

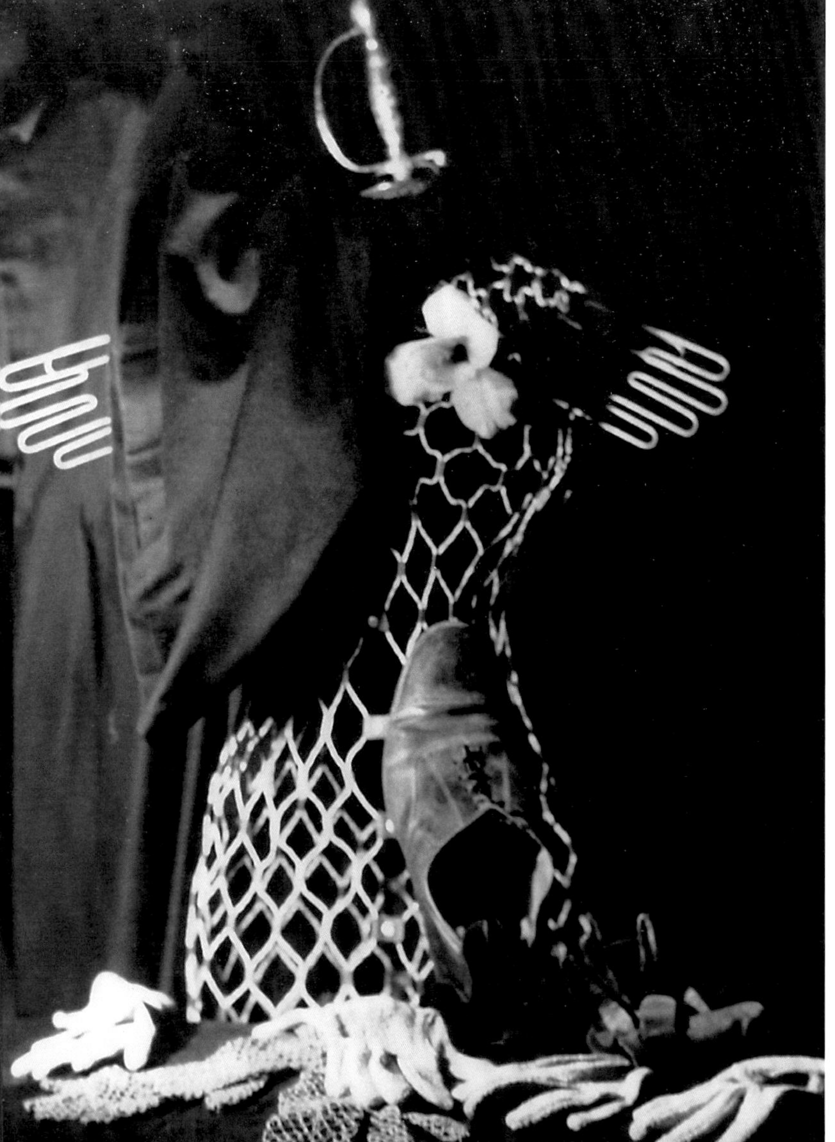

45. Portrait of André Breton and Jacqueline Lamba, 1935.

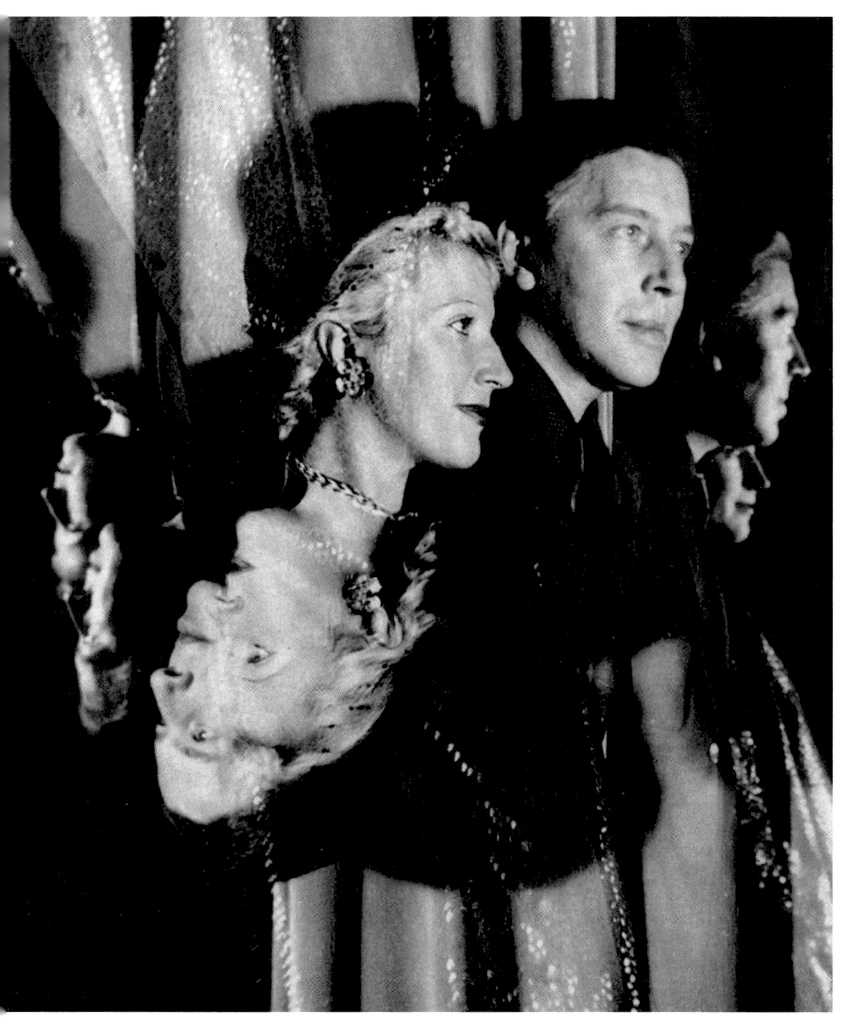

46. *I Bet By Heart*, 1936.

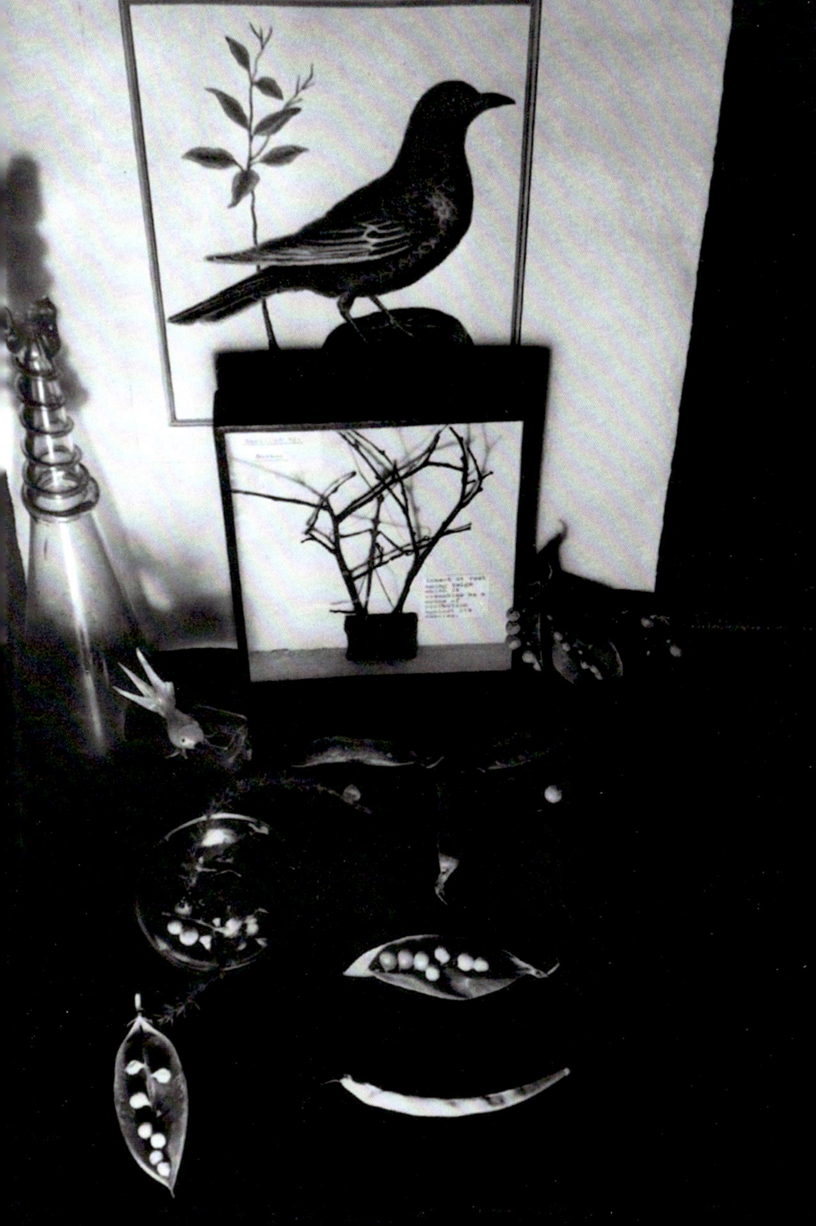

47. 1936.

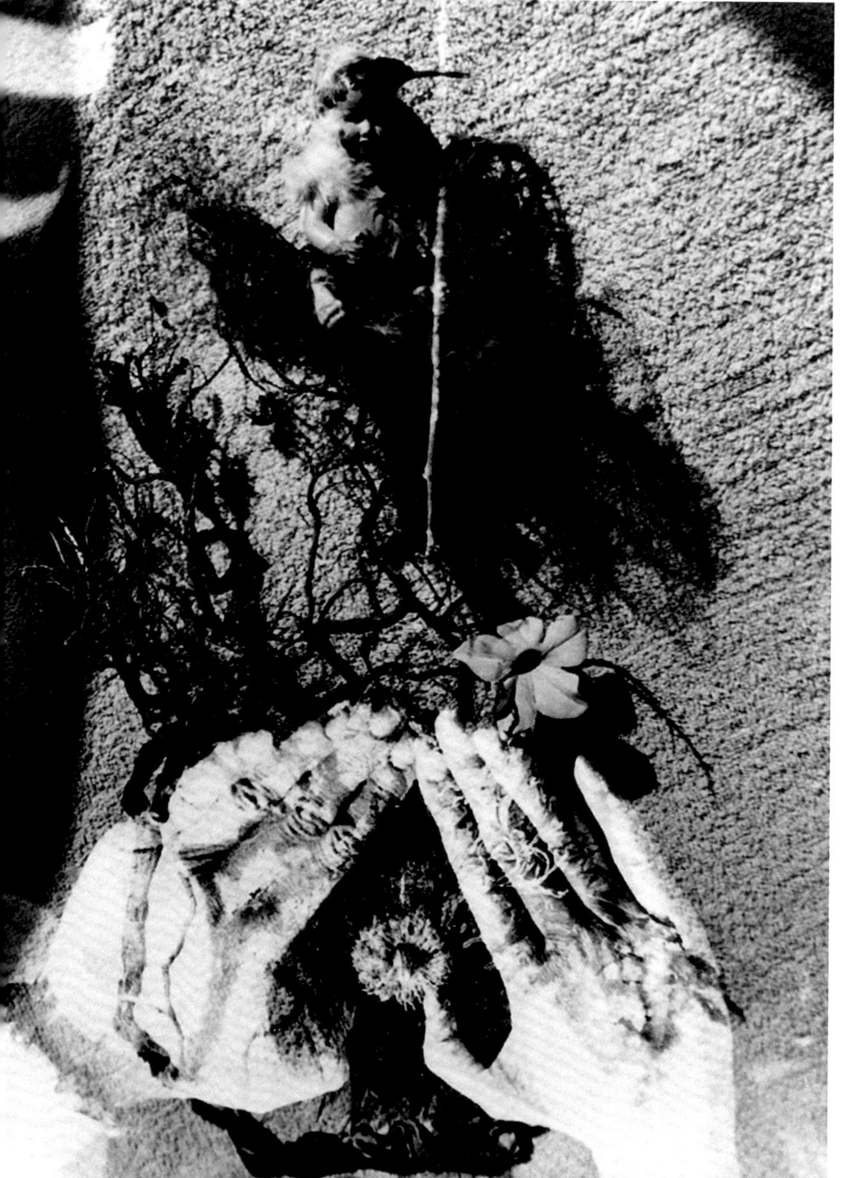

48. *I Would Give My Life*, 1936.

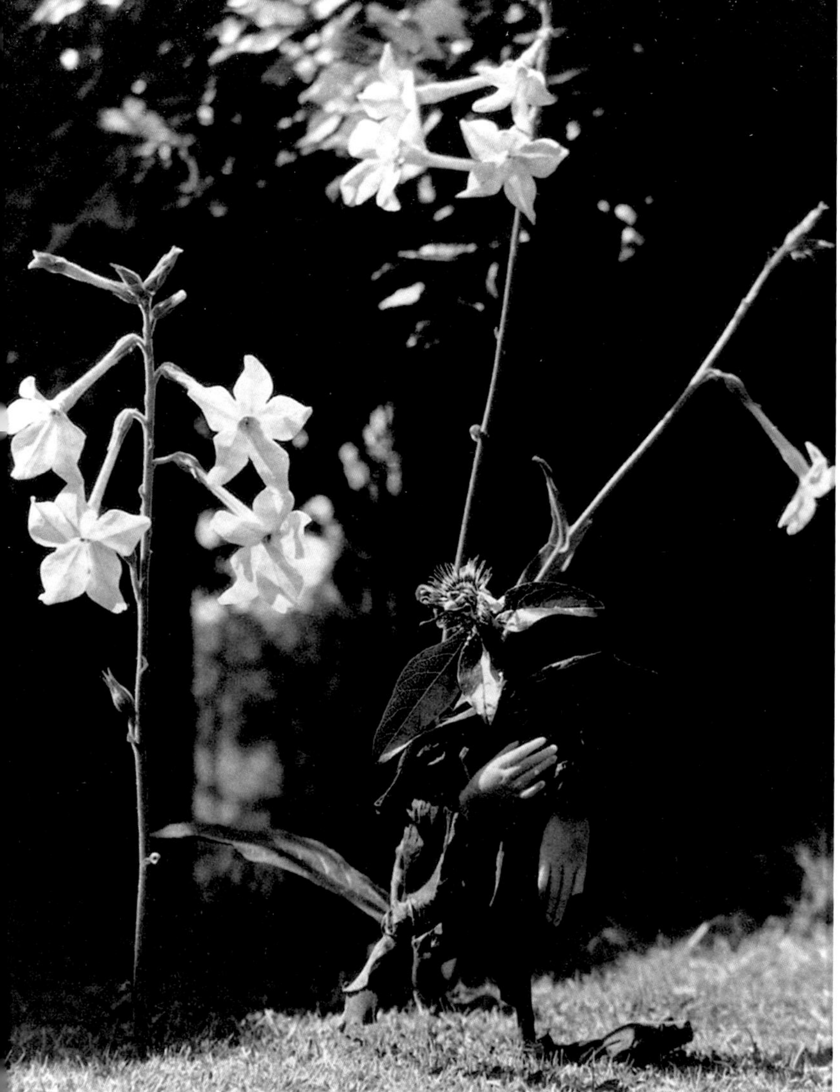

49. 1936.

Plate XVII in *Le Coeur de Pic*,
José Corti, Paris, 1937.

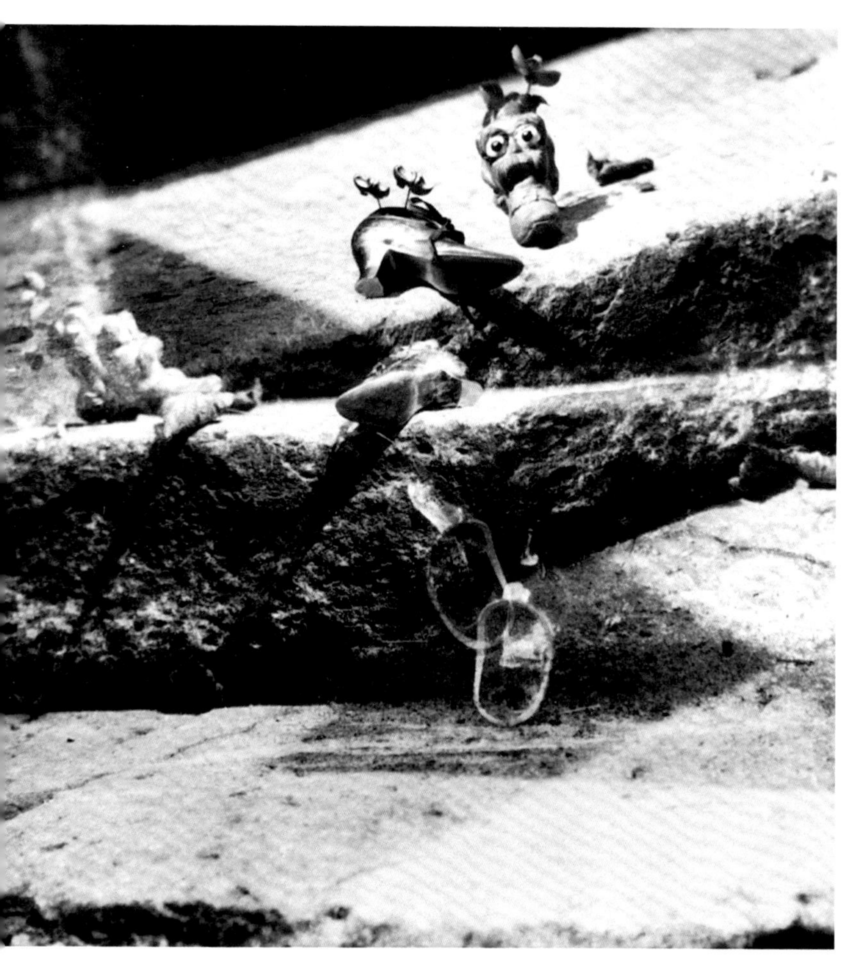

50. 1936.
Plate XV in *Le Coeur de Pic*,
José Corti, Paris, 1937.

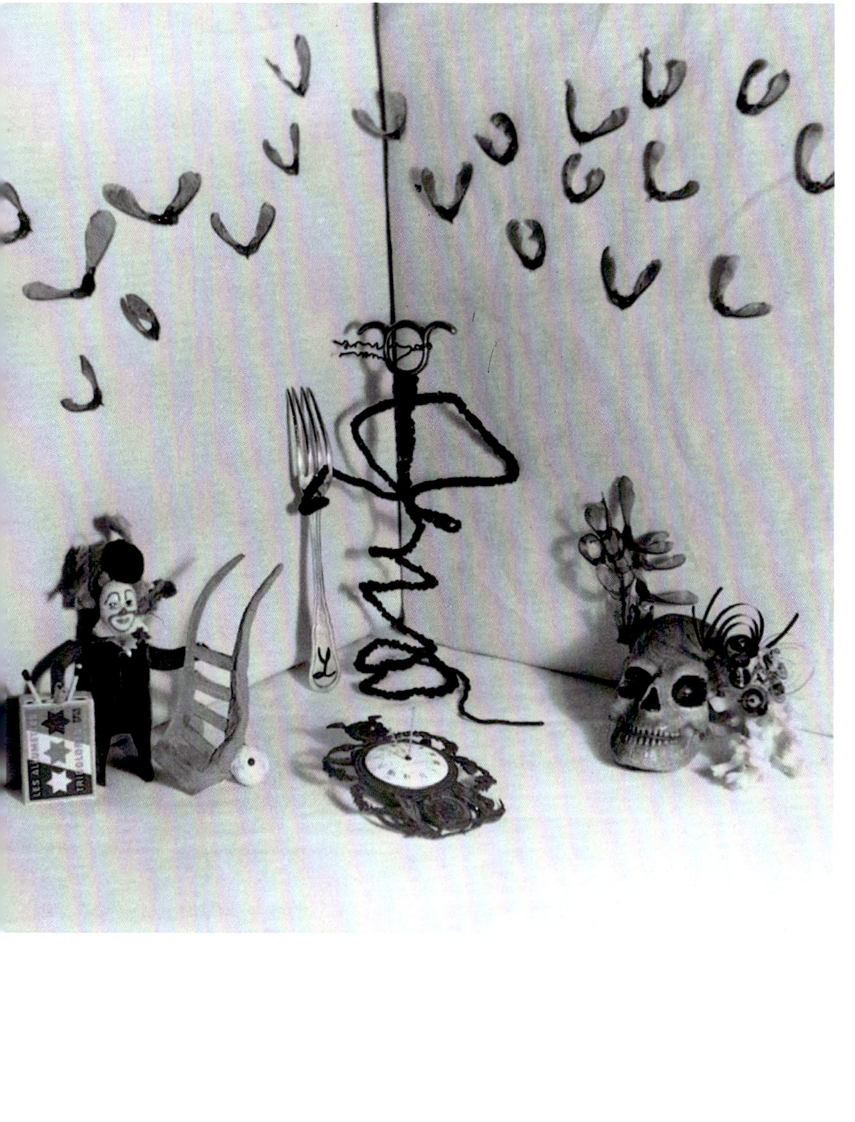

51. *Cotton Grass*, 1936.

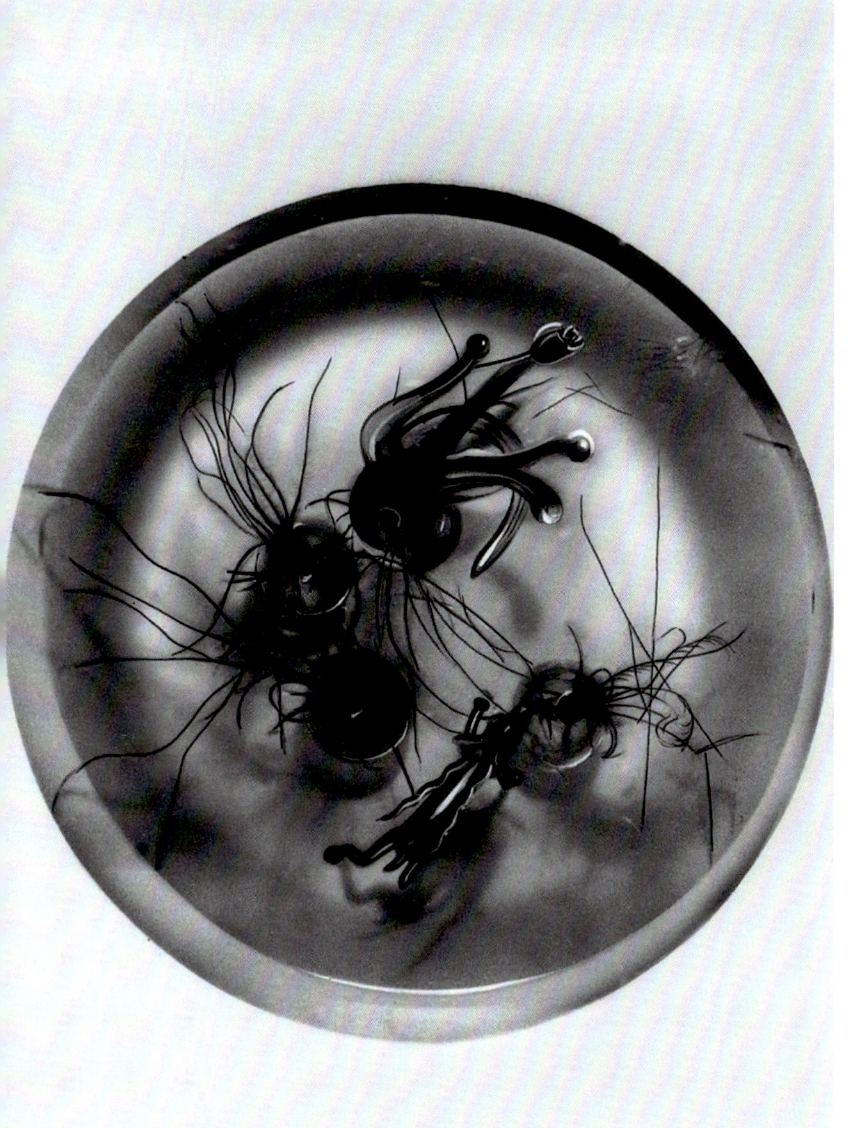

52. 1936.

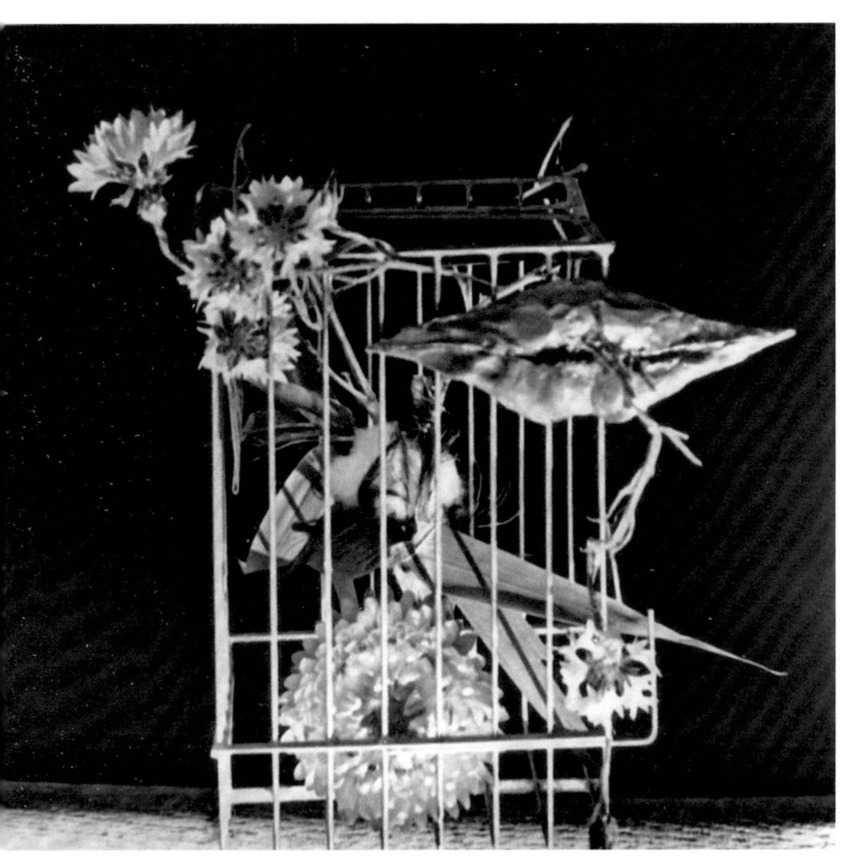

*53. Who Isn't Afraid of the Big, Bad Wolf That
Sets the Boat on its Keel and Sets Sail Adrift*, 1936.

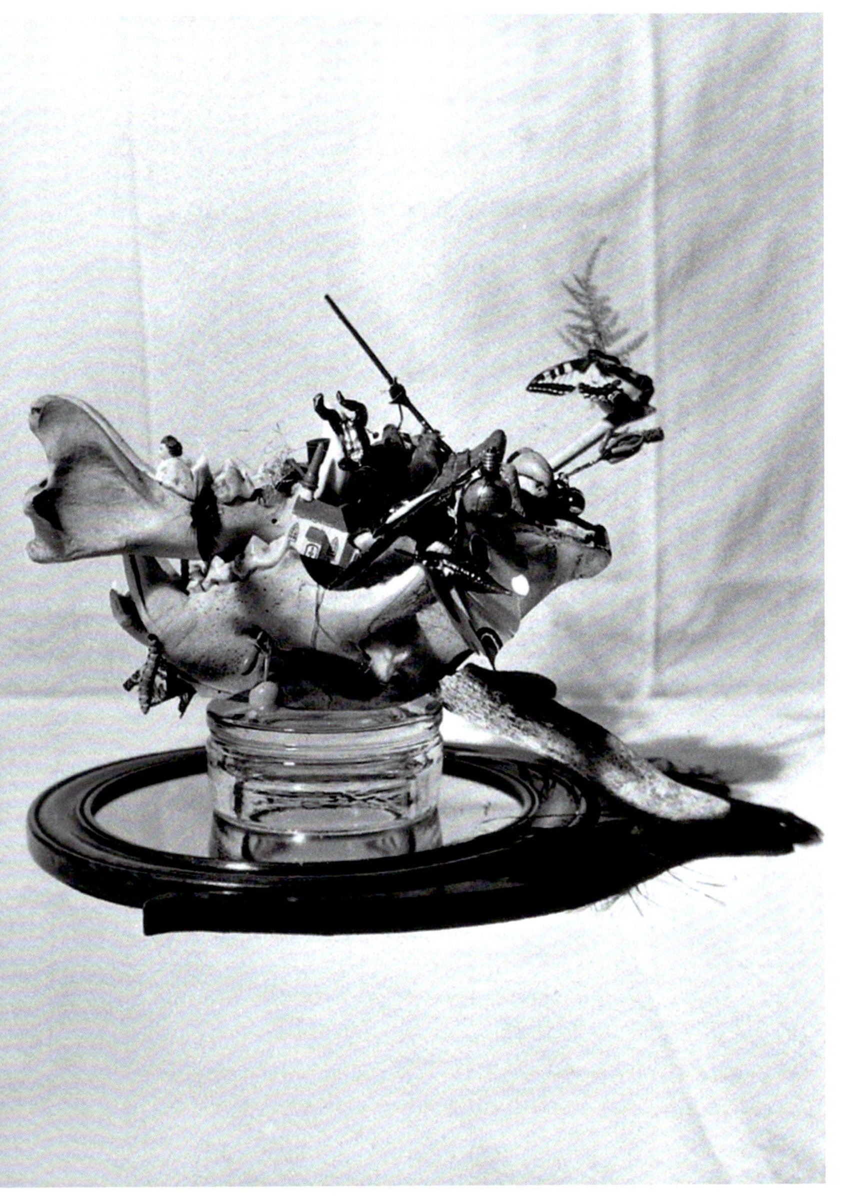

54. 1936.

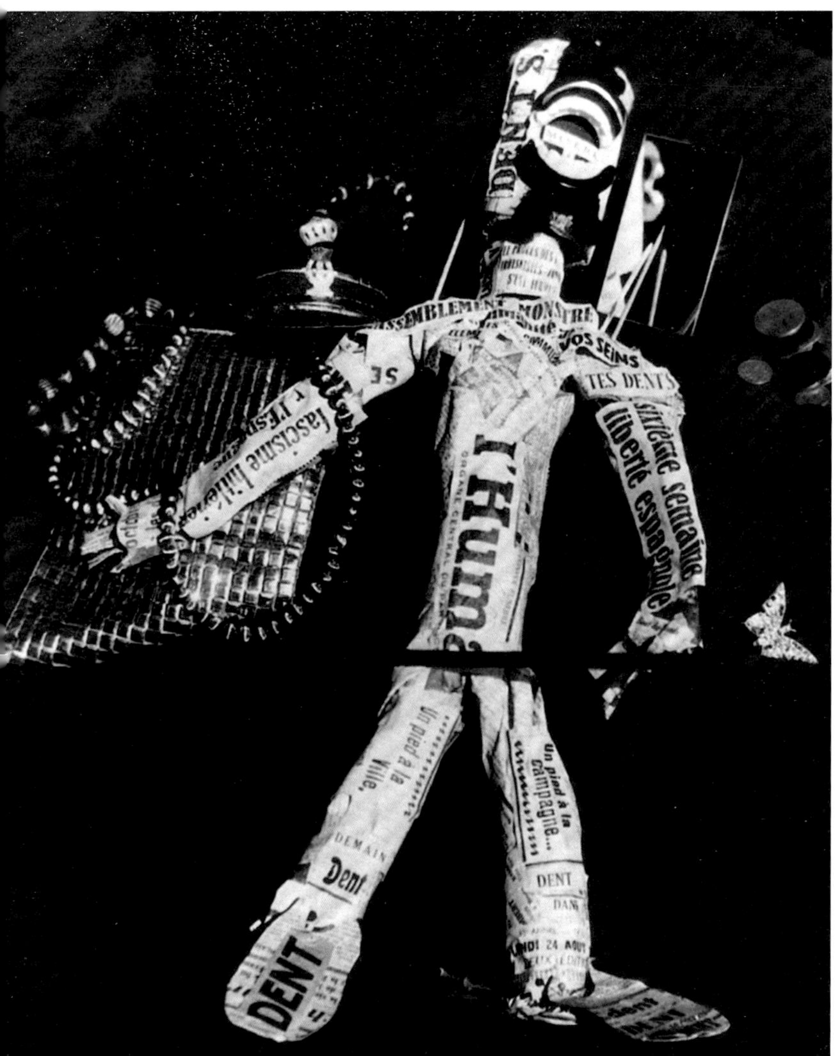

55. *Take a Small Pointed Stick*, 1936.

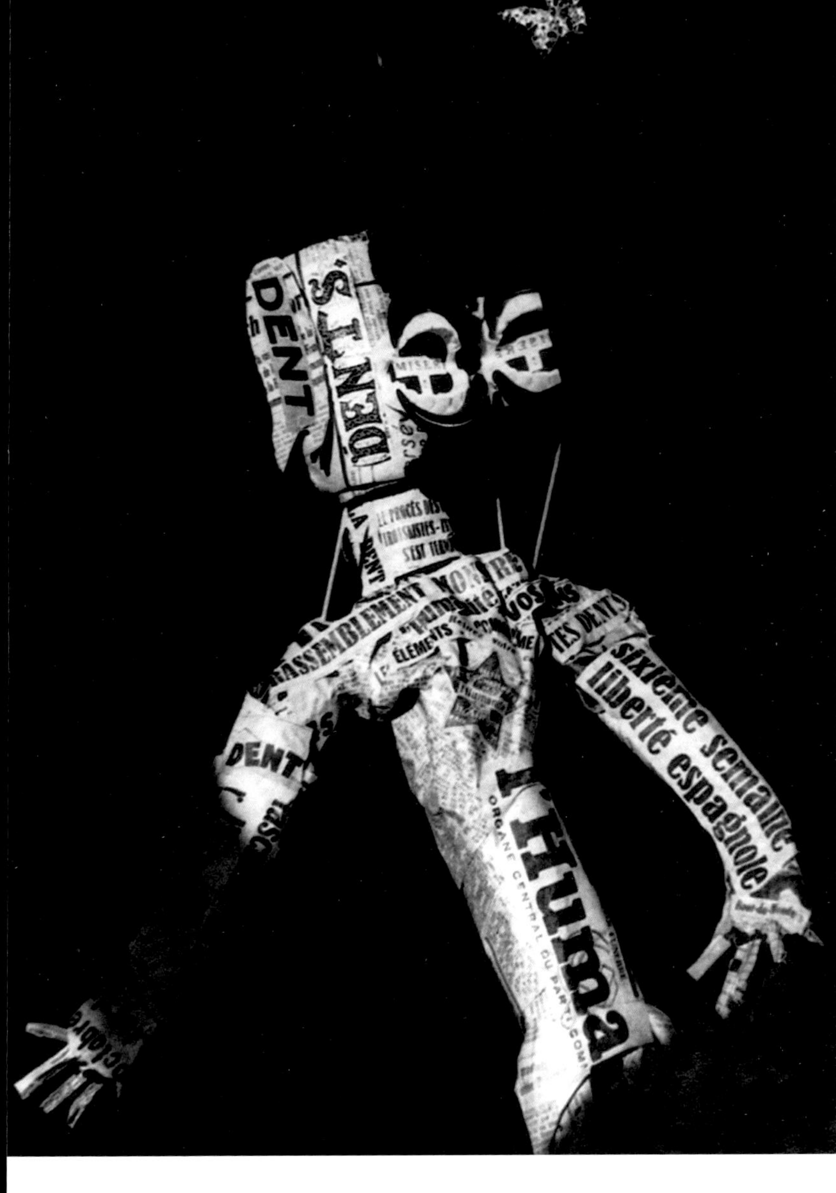

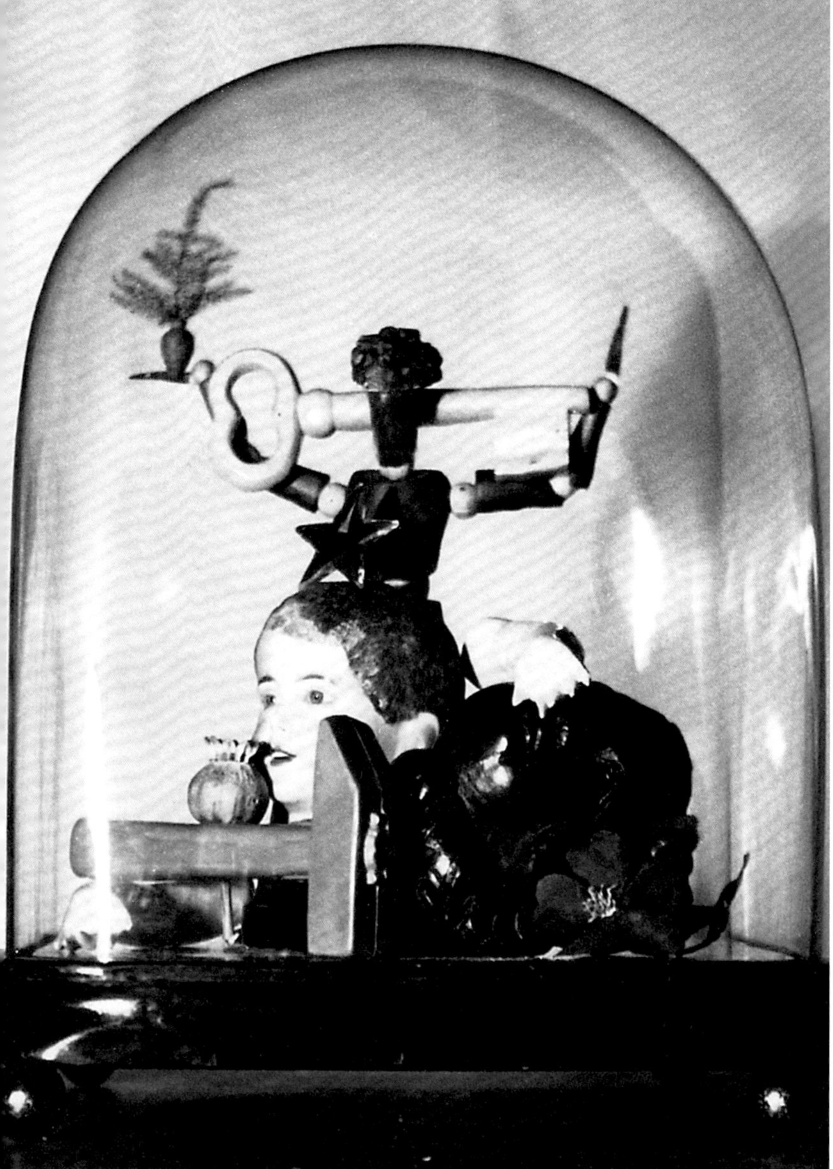

57. *Burnt My Hands While Dying*, c. 1936.

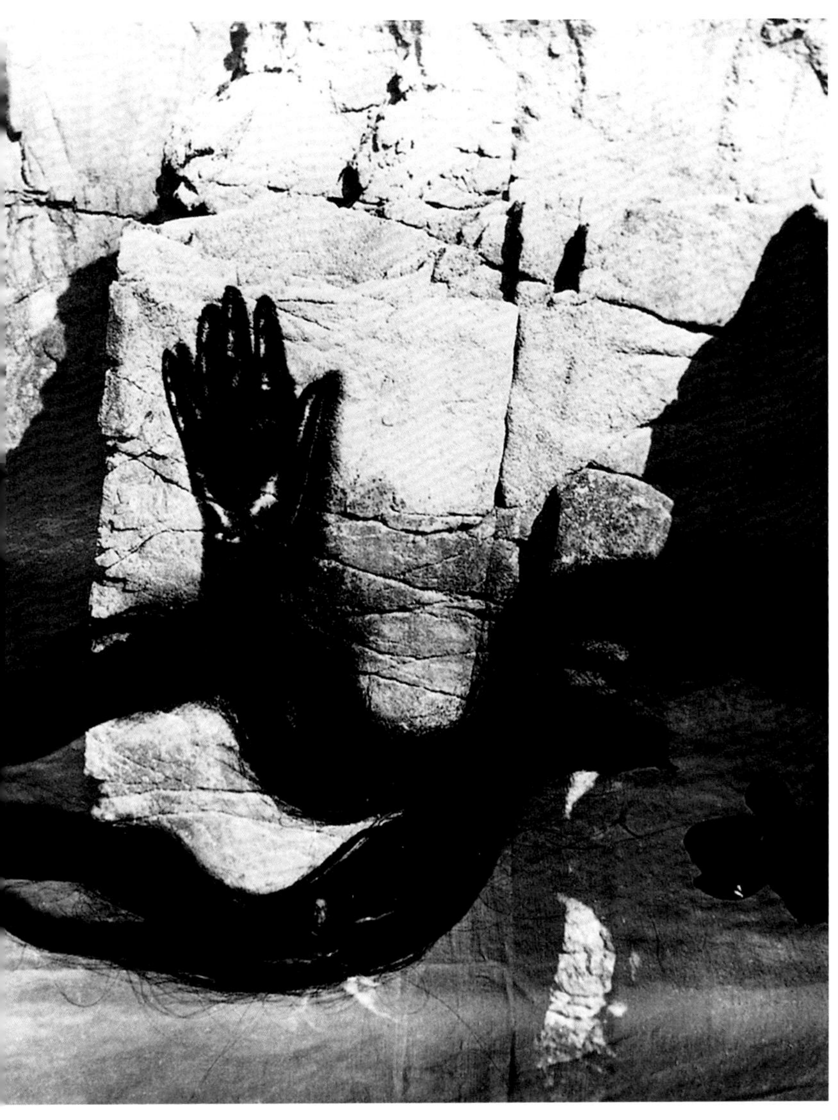

58. c. 1938.

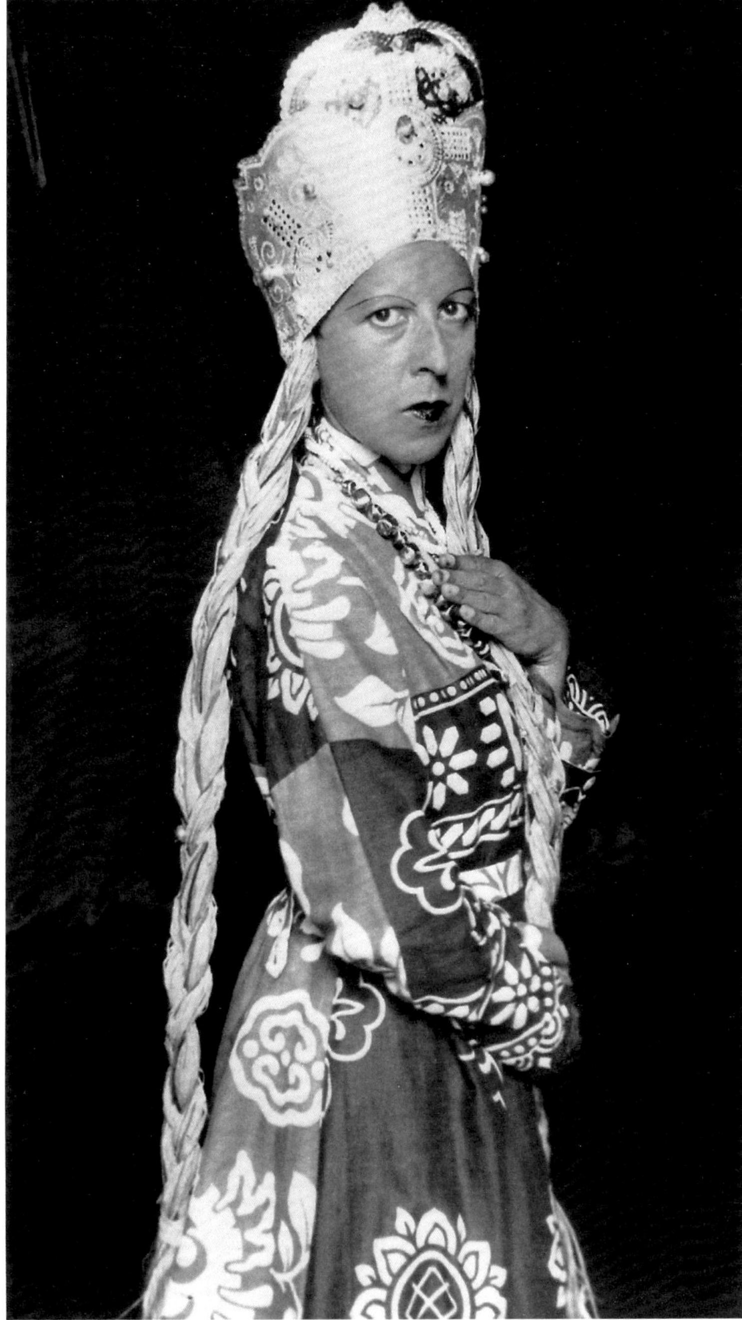

59. c. 1939.

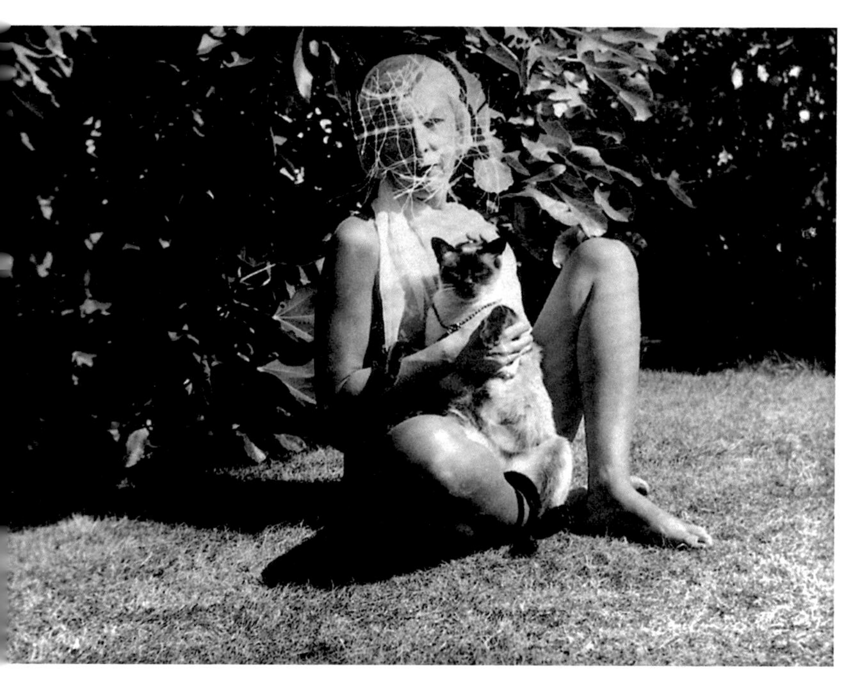

60. c. 1938.

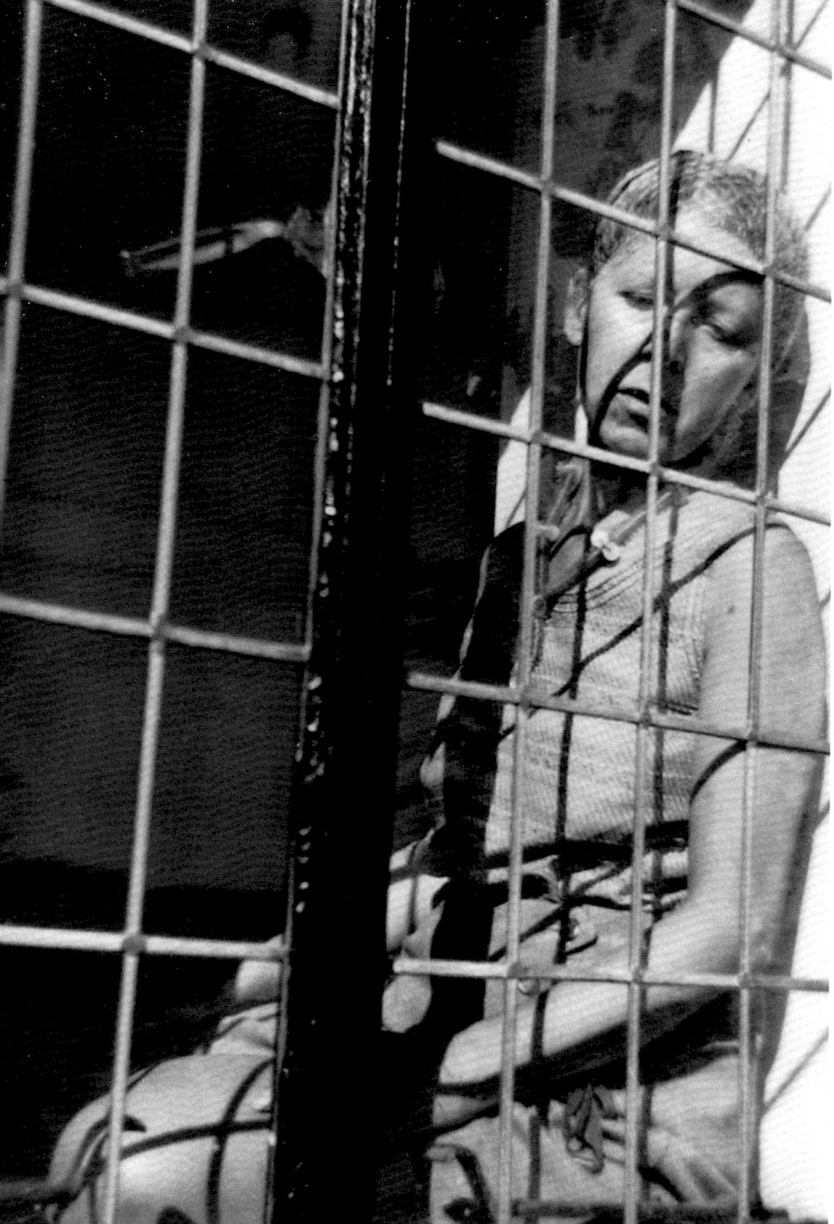

61. Portrait of Jacqueline Lamba, May 1939.

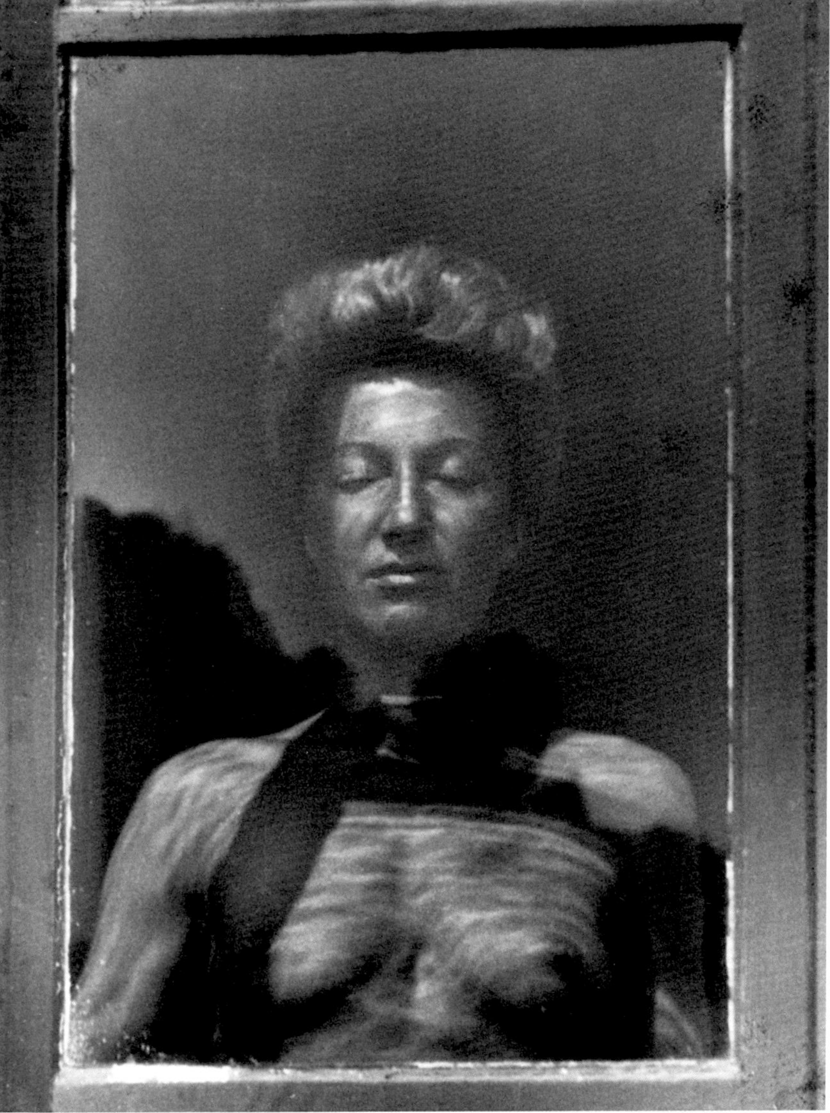

62.1939.

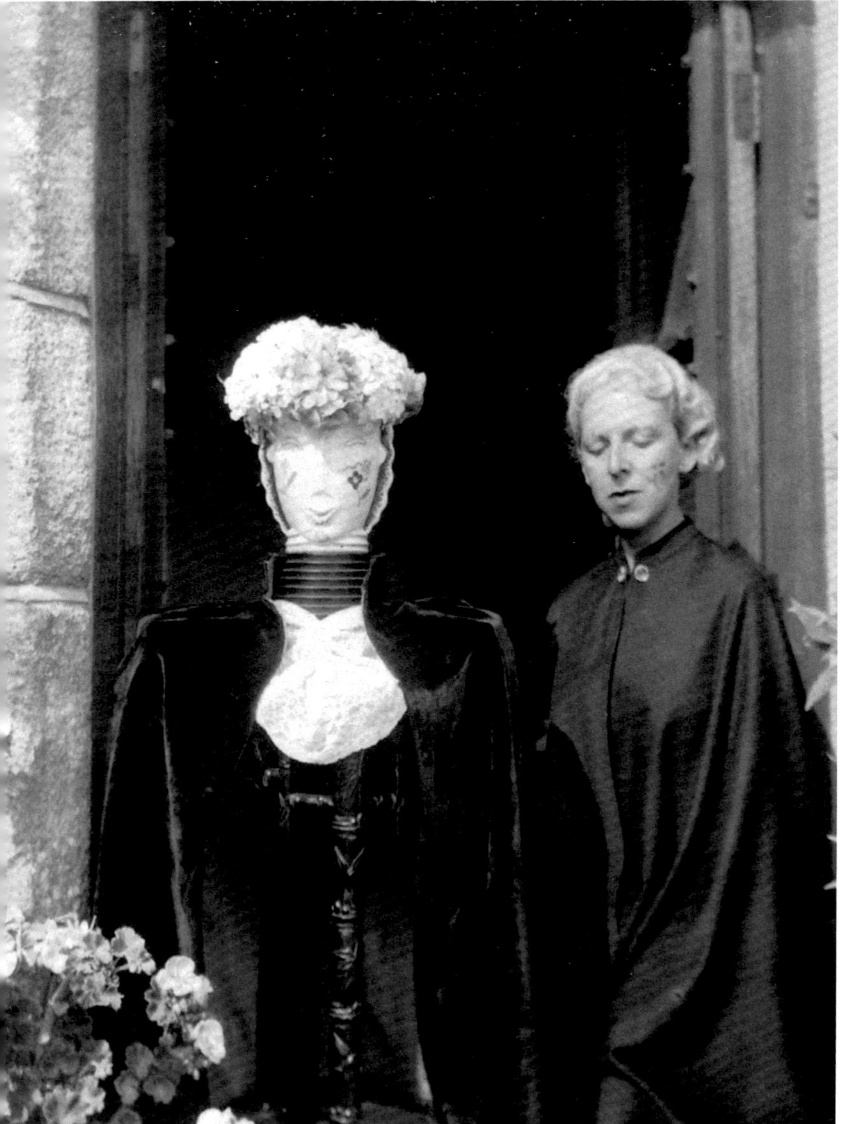

63. 1939.

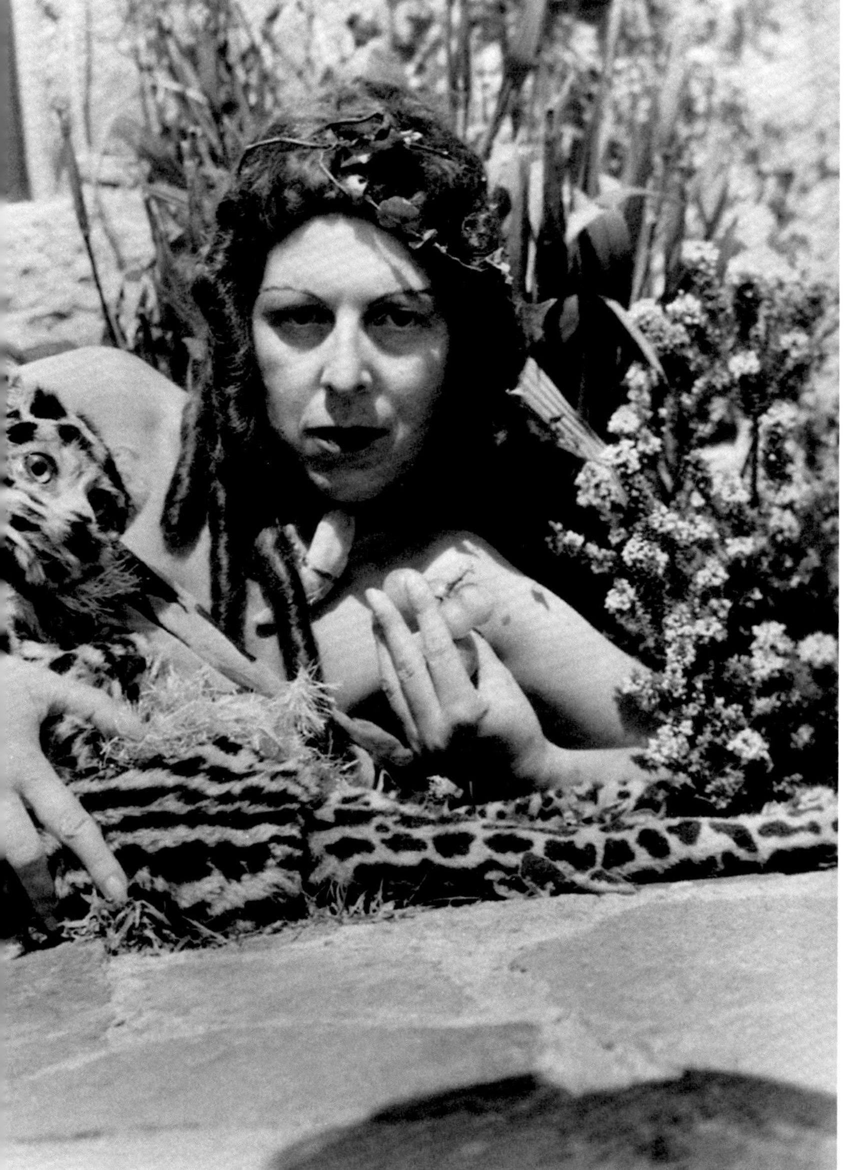

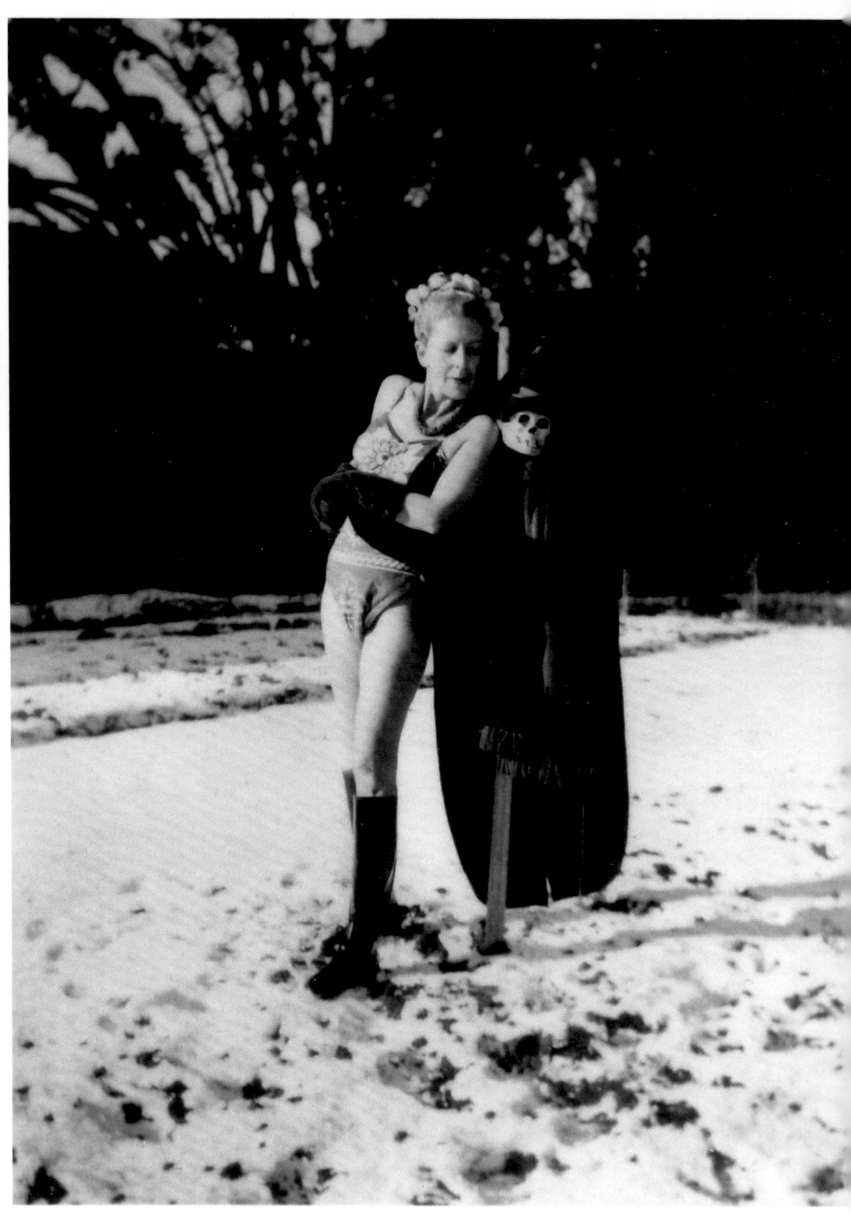

64. 1940.

65. *The Way of Cats V*, c. 1948.

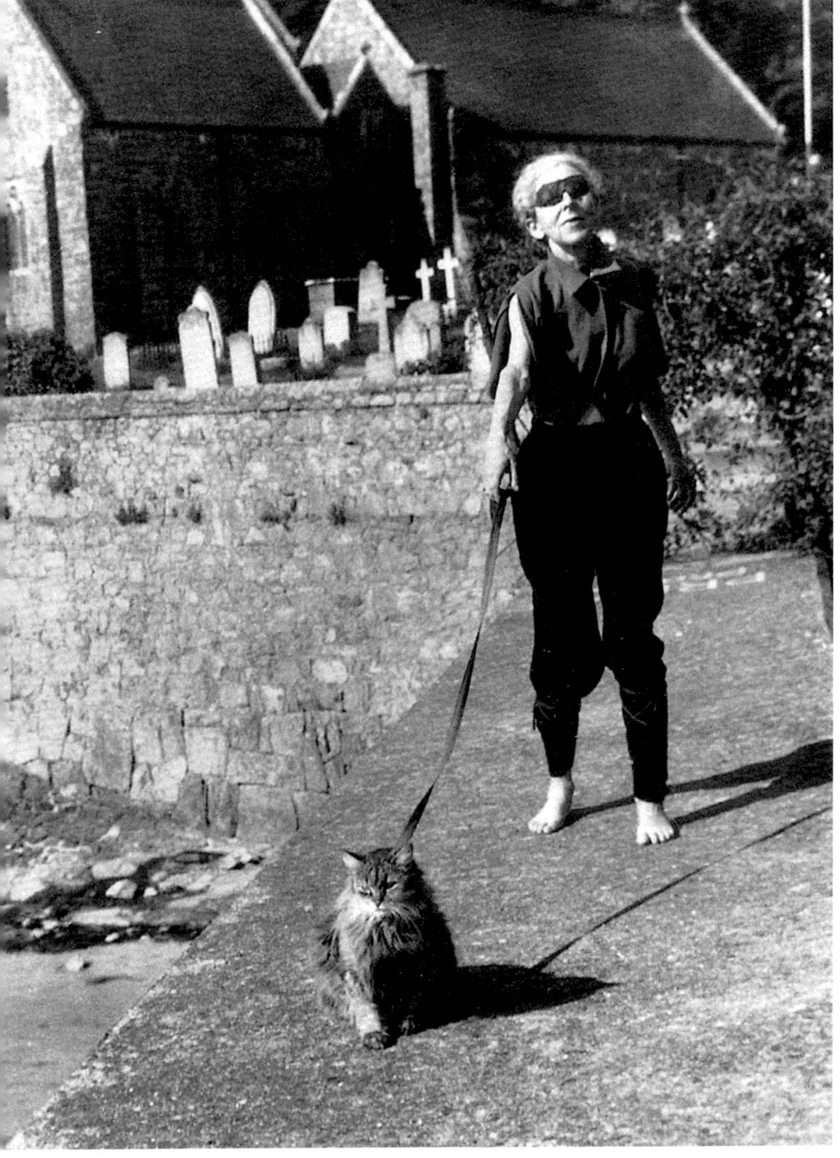

66. *The Tank of the Coronation II*, 1940.

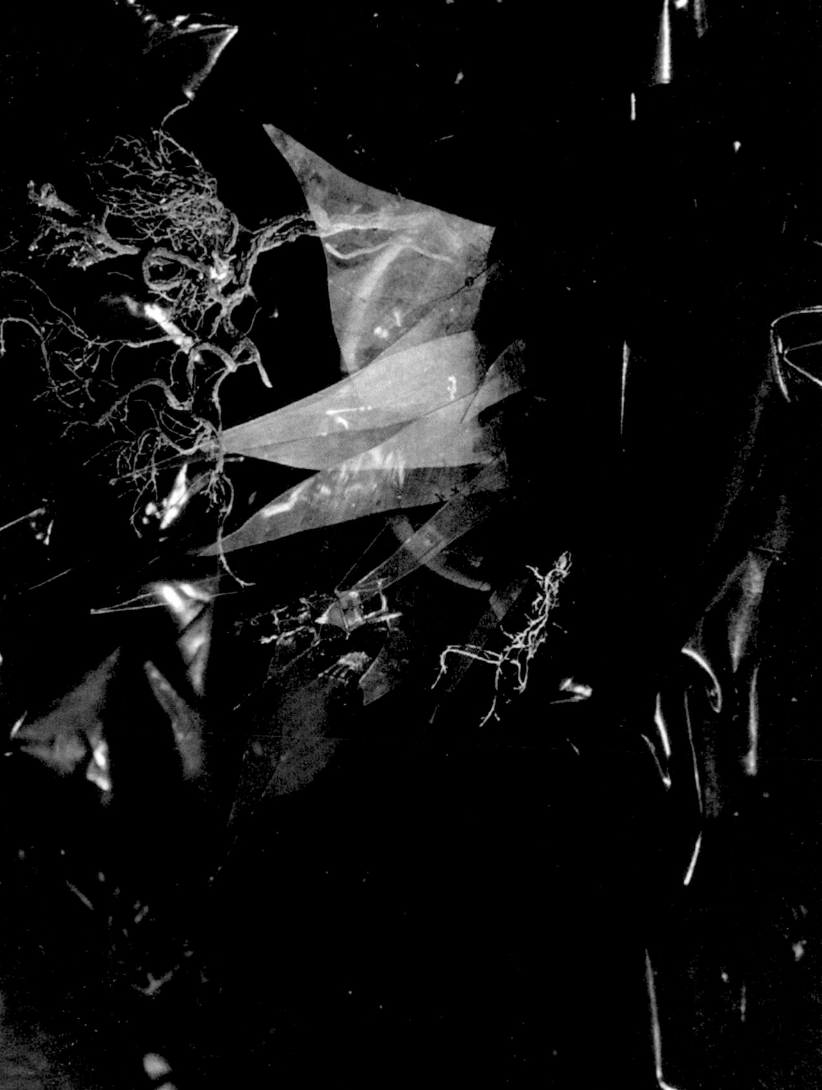

67. c. 1947.

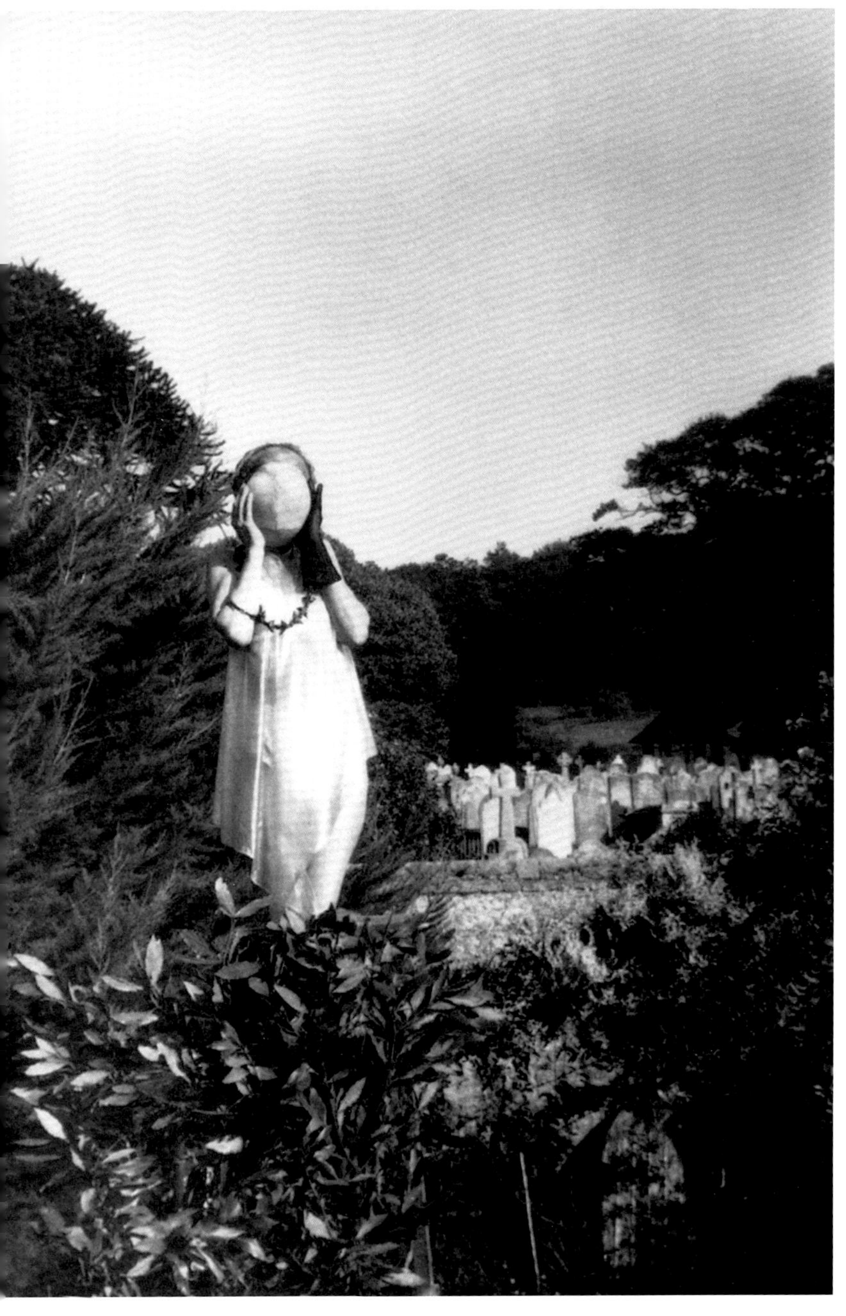

Biography

1894 Born Lucy Schwob in Nantes, France, on 25 October. Niece of Marcel Schwob and great-niece of Léon Cahun.

1905–1909 Attends school in Nantes and in England. Meets Suzanne Malherbe.

1914–1915 First collaboration with the *Mercure de France*. Adopts the pseudonym Claude Cahun. First photographic self-portraits.

1917–1921 Studied literature and philosophy at the Sorbonne. Meets Chana Orloff, Georges Pitoëff, Adrienne Monnier, Sylvia Beach. Publishes *Vues et visions* (1919).

1922 Moves to 70 bis, rue Notre-Dame-des-Champs in Paris, with her life partner Suzanne Malherbe.

1924–1929 Contributes to several literary journals and magazines. Takes photographs. Theatrical work. Becomes acquainted with Henri Michaux (through Jacques Viot), Jane Heap, Pierre Morhange, Pierre Albert-Birot, Georges Ribemont-Dessaignes, Robert Desnos.

1930 Publishes an autobiographical essay, *Aveux non avenus*, illustrated with photomontages created in collaboration with Marcel Moore (Suzanne Malherbe). Anamorphic self-portrait (*Bifur*, no. 5, April 1930).

1932 Joins the Association of Revolutionary Artists and Writers. Meets André Breton and becomes connected with the Surrealists.

1934 Publishes the pamphlet *Les paris sont ouverts* (José Corti). Becomes acquainted with the 'Brunet Group' (Jean Legrand, Néoclès Coutouzis, Pierre Caminade).

1935–1936 Becomes a co-founder of the Contre-Attaque movement, alongside Georges Bataille and André Breton. Socializes with René Crevel, Gaston Ferdière, Tristan Tzara. Meets Jacques Lacan, Salvador Dalí, Lise Deharme. Creates some Surrealist objects. Intense period of photographic work.

1937 *Le Coeur de Pic* (José Corti), 20 photographs to accompany poems by Lise Deharme. Buys a house, La Rocquaise, on the island of Jersey. Claude Cahun and Suzanne Malherbe leave Paris permanently.

1940–1945 Creates anti-Nazi counter-propaganda and engages in acts of resistance against Jersey's German occupiers. Arrested and sentenced to death, Claude Cahun and Suzanne Malherbe narrowly escape execution. Some of her work is destroyed during the war.

1945–1954 Re-establishes contact with Henri Michaux, André Breton and other Surrealists. Short stays in Paris. Edits *Confidences au miroir*. Final photographic self-portraits.

1954 Claude Cahun dies in St Helier, Jersey, on 8 December 1954. Claude Cahun's principal archives are conserved by the Jersey Heritage Trust and the Musée des Beaux-Arts, Nantes.

Selected Bibliography

Major publications

1913–1914 'Chroniques', illustrated by Marcel Moore, *Le Phare de la Loire*.

1919 *Vues et visions*, illustrated by Marcel Moore, Georges Crès, Paris

1921 'L'Idée-maîtresse (I–IV)', *La Gerbe*, nos. 29–32, February–May

1925 'Héroïnes', *Le Mercure de France*, no. 639, February. New ed.: 1001 nuits, Paris, 2006
'Méditation de mademoiselle Lucy Schwob', *Philosophies*, no. 5/6, March
'Récits de rêve', *Le Disque vert*, year 3, series 4, no. 2
'La Sadique Judith', *Mercure de France*, no. 639, February. New ed.: *Pleine Marge*, no. 14, December 1991

1926 'Carnaval en chambre', *La ligne de coeur*, book 4, March

1930 *Aveux non avenus*, with 10 photomontages, Éditions du Carrefour, Paris. New ed.: 1001 nuits, Paris, 2011
'Frontière humaine', photographic self-portrait, *Bifur*, no. 5, April

1934 *Les paris sont ouverts*, José Corti, Paris.

1936 'Prenez garde aux objets domestiques', *Cahiers d'art*, June

1937 Lise Deharme, *Le Coeur de Pic*, 20 photographs by Claude Cahun, José Corti, Paris. New ed.: MeMo, Nantes, 2004

1992 *Ballon captif*, Éditions Myrddin, Brive

1994 *Mise en scène: Claude Cahun, Tacita Dean, Virginia Nimarkoh*, text by David Bate and François Leperlier, Institute of Contemporary Arts, London

1999 *Claude Cahun*, 'Photo Poche', no. 85, Nathan, Paris. New ed.: Actes Sud, Arles, 2011, 2023

2002 *Écrits*, edited with introduction by François Leperlier, Jean-Michel Place, Paris

2008 *Disavowals: or Cancelled Confessions*, MIT Press, Cambridge, MA

2011 François Leperlier, Juan Vicente Aliaga, *Claude Cahun*, Hazan, Paris

2022 *Il y a mode et mode*, with Marcel Moore, Jean-Michel Place, Paris

Critical works

1934 André Breton, *Qu'est-ce que le surréalisme?*, René Henriquez, Brussels

1978 Gaston Ferdière, *Les Mauvaises Fréquentations*, Jean-Claude Simoën, Paris

1982 Édouard Jaguer, *Les Mystères de la chambre noire: Le surréalisme et la photographie*, Flammarion, Paris

1985 Rosalind Krauss, Jane Livingston, Dawn Ades, *L'amour fou: Photography & Surrealism*, Corcoran Gallery of Art, Washington DC

1991 François Leperlier, 'Claude Cahun', *Pleine Marge*, no. 14, December

1994 François Leperlier, 'La gravité des apparences', in *Le Rêve d'une ville. Nantes et le surréalisme*, Musée des Beaux-Arts, Nantes; Réunion des Musées Nationaux, Paris

1998 François Leperlier, 'L'assomption de Claude Cahun', in Georgiana Colvile & Katharine Conley (eds.), *La femme s'entête. La part du féminin dans le surréalisme*, Lachenal & Ritter, Paris

1992 Honor Lasalle & Abigail Solomon-Godeau, 'Surrealist Confession: Claude Cahun's Photomontages', *Afterimage*, vol. 19, March

1993 Jennifer Blessing, 'Resisting, Determination: An Introduction to the Work of Claude Cahun, Surrealist Artist and Writer', *Found Object*, no. 1, City University of New York

1994 Michel Frizot, *Nouvelle histoire de la photographie*, Bordas/Adam Biro, Paris

1995 Élisabeth Lebovici, 'I Am Training Don't Kiss Me', in *Claude Cahun photographe*, Jean-Michel Place/Paris Musées, Paris

1997 Christian Bouqueret, *Des années folles aux années noires. La nouvelle vision photographique en France, 1920–1940*, Marval, Paris

Dirk Snauwaert, François Leperlier *et al.*, *Claude Cahun: Bilder*, Schirmer/Mosel, Munich

1998 Whitney Chadwick & Dawn Ades (eds.), *Mirror Images: Women, Surrealism, and Self-Representation*, MIT Press, Cambridge, MA

1999 Shelley Rice (ed.), *Inverted Odysseys: Claude Cahun, Maya Deren, Cindy Sherman*, MIT Press, Cambridge, MA

2006 Louise Downie, *Don't Kiss Me: The Art of Claude Cahun and Marcel Moore*, Aperture, New York; Tate Publishing, London
François Leperlier, *Claude Cahun: L'Exotisme intérieur*, Fayard, Paris

2007 Gen Doy, *Claude Cahun: A Sensual Politics of Photography*, I. B. Tauris, London & New York

2015 Agnès Martetteau, Blandine Chavanne *et al.*, *Claude Cahun et ses doubles*, MeMo, Nantes

2017 Jennifer L. Shaw, *Exist Otherwise: The Life and Works of Claude Cahun*, Reaktion Books, London

Films

2006 Lizzie Thynne, *Playing a Part: The Story of Claude Cahun*, 45 mins.
Barbara Hammer, *Lover Other: The Story of Claude Cahun and Marcel Moore*, 55 mins.

Theatre

2002 Andrea Kleine, *Claude*, Dance Theater Workshop, The Duke on 42nd Street, New York

Selected Exhibitions

Solo exhibitions

1980 *Claude Cahun*, Galerie Claude Givaudan, Geneva.

1992 *Claude Cahun*, Galerie Zabriskie, New York.
Claude Cahun: photographies des années 20 et 30, Galerie Zabriskie, Paris.

1993 *Claude Cahun et Suzanne Malherbe*, Jersey Museum, St Helier.

1995 *Claude Cahun 1894–1954*, Musée d'Art Moderne de la Ville de Paris.
Claude Cahun, Espace Berggruen, Paris.

1997 *Claude Cahun*, Ginza Artspace, Tokyo.
Claude Cahun, Neue Pinakothek, Munich.
Claude Cahun, Neue Galerie am Landesmuseum Joanneum, Graz.
Claude Cahun, Museum Folkwang, Essen.

1998 *Claude Cahun photographe*, Museum Folkwang, Essen.
Don't Kiss Me – Disruptions of the Self in the Work of Claude Cahun, Presentation House Gallery, Vancouver.

1999 *Don't Kiss Me – Disruptions of the Self in the Work of Claude Cahun*, Art Gallery of Ontario, Toronto.

2001 *Claude Cahun*, Instituto Valenciano de Arte Moderno, Valencia.

2005 *Acting Out: Claude Cahun and Marcel Moore*, The Judah L. Magnes Museum, University of California, Berkeley, CA; Colby College Museum of Art, Waterville, ME; Jersey Museum, St Helier.

2011 *Claude Cahun/Sue Tompkins*, Inverleith House, Edinburgh.

2011–2012 *Claude Cahun*, Jeu de Paume, Paris; La Virreina Centre de la Imatge, Barcelona; Art Institute of Chicago.

2015 *Claude Cahun. Photographies, dessins, écrits*, Bibliothèque Municipale, Nantes.

2022 *Claude Cahun: Under the Skin*, Kunsthal, Rotterdam.

Group exhibitions

1985 *L'Amour fou: Photography and Surrealism*, Corcoran Gallery of Art, Washington DC.
Explosante-fixe. Photographie et surréalisme, Centre Pompidou, Paris.

1991 *Paris des années trente. Le surréalisme et le livre*, Galerie Zabriskie, Paris.
Photographie et sculpture, Centre National de la Photographie, Paris.

1994 *Mise en scène*, Institute of Contemporary Art, London.
Le Rêve d'une ville. Nantes et le surréalisme, Musée des Beaux-Arts de Nantes.

1995 *Féminin masculin*, Centre Pompidou, Paris.

1996 *Inside the Visible*, Institute of Contemporary Art, Boston.
Rrose Is A Rrose Is A Rrose, Guggenheim Museum, New York.

1997 *Double vie–double vue*, Fondation Cartier, Paris.
Floating Images of Women in Art History, Tochigi Prefectural Museum, Utsunomiya.
El Rostro Velado, Koldo Mitxelena Kulturunea, San Sebastian, Spain.

1999–2000 *Inverted Odysseys: Claude Cahun, Maya Deren, Cindy Sherman*, Grey Art Gallery, New York.

2000 *Inverted Odysseys: Claude Cahun, Maya Deren, Cindy Sherman*, Museum of Contemporary Art, Miami.

2001 *Surrealism: Desire Unbound*, Tate Modern, London.

2002 *La Révolution surréaliste*, Centre Pompidou, Paris.

The Photofile series is the original English-language edition of the Photo Poche collection. It was first published between 1986 and 1992 by the Centre National de la Photographie, Paris, with the support of the French Ministry of Culture. Robert Delpire (1926–2017) was the creator of the series and its managing editor until 2017.

General editors: Géraldine Lay and François Leperlier

Series design by Matthew Young

Translated from the French by Jill Phythian

First published in the United Kingdom in 2023 by
Thames & Hudson Ltd, 181A High Holborn, London WC1V 7QX

First published in the United States of America in 2023 by
Thames & Hudson Inc., 500 Fifth Avenue, New York, New York 10110

British Library Cataloguing-in-Publication Data
A catalogue record for this book is available from the British Library

Library of Congress Control Number 2023933243

ISBN 978-0-500-29749-0

Printed and bound in Italy

Be the first to know about our new releases, exclusive content and author events by visiting
thamesandhudson.com
thamesandhudsonusa.com
thamesandhudson.com.au